THE FORTH-C MING CRISIS

ANDRÉ JOHNSON

THE FORTH-C⊙MING CRISIS

INSPIRED
PUBLISHING

The Forthcoming Crisis
First Edition, First Impression 2020
ISBN 978-1-990961-37-3
Copyright © Andre Johnson

Published by:
Inspired Publishing
PO Box 82058 | Southdale | 2135
Johannesburg , South Africa
Email: info@inspiredpublishing.co.za
www.inspiredpublishing.co.za

CONTENTS

DEDICATION

Firstly, all thanks, praise and adoration go to my Heavenly Father for the support, strength, wisdom, and health he has bestowed me during this time of writing the book

Secondly, as cited by our President Ramaphosa: *"Most of our health facilities have proven resilient, capable and able to withstand and deal with the surge.*

The modelled projections of infections, hospitalisation and deaths have had to be adjusted downwards as we have recorded better progress in the management of the disease.

The progress we are recording in our management of COVID 19 would not be possible without the dedication and professionalism of our doctors, nurses, and other health personnel, who have had to confront this unprecedented disease often under extremely difficult conditions.

We pay tribute to them, many of whom have been infected and some who have lost their lives taking care of others.

None of this would have been possible without all the other frontline workers, policewomen and men, soldiers, traffic officials and volunteers who have been at the forefront of our national response.

We also pay tribute to our medical experts in various health institutions, such as the National Health Laboratory Service, National Institute for Communicable Diseases, Medical Research Council and the Ministerial Advisory Committee who continue to play an invaluable role in our management of COVID-19" (Notice, 2020a).

ACKNOWLEDGEMENTS

The SHERQ and Wellness Team – without your expertise, perseverance, commitment, and dedication, implementing this system would not be possible. Thank you for your value-based leadership, you make the country proud.

For all the Endorsements & Foreword – I want to praise and thank you from the depth of my heart for all the kind words you wrote in support of this book and cause. May God Bless you and thanks for your recognition.

Then my family, my Mom and specifically my wife Patty who supported me as well as my children who had to endure with an emotional and physical absent Father and husband during the last 5 months of writing this book and his commitment during the Pandemic.

I dedicate this book to the **South African Mining Industry** with their continuous efforts to assist with the Crisis and to all those that have lost their lives due to Covid-19.

Lastly "without Faith it is impossible to please GOD". Thanks, and gratitude to our Church and its leaders who supported me during this period, with words of strength, commitment and support.

ENDORSEMENTS

Covid 19 has caused physical harm to many people but studies show that the emotional health of people might have suffered more. In the world there is now a high level of stress, fear, anxiety, depression, gender violence and in China the divorce rate has increased a great deal. In this book Johnson addresses not only the obvious business strategies that are important for the Health and Safety practitioner to help the company to flourish, but with his extensive experience in this field he shows scientifically yet also practically how the practitioner can use this pandemic to help his company to excel.

Emotional intelligence determines the success of leaders. He shows how emotional intelligence should also be part of the repertoire of the practitioner. He shows how to get off the bench with the team and take control of their goals and vision and to live a stressless, fearless life. WIN THE DAY! There are many books on leaders but only a few that strip away theoretical jargon and focuses on what you need to know and put into practice to be a successful leader. He emphasises how a servant leader, by serving others, will eventually help enhance the success and performance of the company. His religious and ethical values make an incredibly special contribution to this book.

I have no doubt that this book is a well needed addition to help the Health and Safety practitioner in these challenging times and will inspire many!

Dr Pieter van Jaarsveld. CEO of Tandem Training, psychologist, and author.

Andre has written a timely book, that honestly explores his journey, struggles and learnings through a pandemic. COVID 19 upended the world and multiple crises ensued. From health to financial, social to workplace the impacts have been felt and we all have had to re-evaluate how we navigate the world we inhabit.

Andre takes us through his journey with candour and deep reflection. As a COVID 19 Compliance Officer in the mining industry he had to step outside of the panic and carve a path that would bring stability to his workplace and the confidence of the people he leads and engages with.

This has not been an easy road for any of us and Andre honestly acknowledges his own need to learn skills on the fly to manage the crisis at work and in his personal life.

While learning the fundamental epidemiology of the virus to taking a course in contact tracing, from drawing on his MBA learnings to implementing sound management principles, he appreciated the importance of validating the fears, beliefs, values, needs and wants of the individual employees, he describes how authentic acknowledgment of individual concerns was the key to building consensus and trust.

With understanding and empathy Andre and his team build a new normal within the workplace.

He shares strategies he employed to create common understanding and goals, to move through the pandemic with a resilience mind set.

The key learnings:

- leveraging diversity of views and perceptions to deliberate and develop a political, economic, social, technological, legal, and environmental (PESTLE) framework. This framework initiates integrated action and pluralistic thinking.

- Using the Viable Systems Modelling (VSM) in the ''what if '' scenario planning to ensure business continuity

- the importance of effective coordination between the services and production departments to ensure consistent production results.

▫ the critical value of on the ground engagement through interventions such as roadshows or Visible Felt Leadership. Listening to the views of the employees and to integrate these into a stakeholder driven response

Against the backdrop of this pandemic he had to undergo his own loss within his family and reach deeply into his spiritual life to continue with the important tasks of managing Health and Safety within his organisation. While this is a personal account, the messages and insights will be of benefit to management and leadership in the time of crisis and calm.

Knowing and working with Andre for many years it has been a privilege to review and recommend this book as it has enormous value in the workplace today and in the future.

Karyn Taylor

Wellness and Disease Management Specialist KT Taylor Consulting

Organizations experience change in many ways, the only constant is change itself, and it is expected by stakeholders that the organization manage the change in a due diligent manner. Many a change is planned and therefor the management of such provides the "luxury" of being more pro-active in the approach with reasonable time frames and schedules; whilst the unplanned change can disrupt the approach totally leaving the responsible people feeling isolated, unsure, overwhelmed and without any support.

Safety practitioners across the globe have found them in such situations and had to rely on their past experience, colleagues in the field, Google, books, letters, papers and write ups to obtain direction and solutions whilst keeping production going and all stakeholders happy – ultimately ensuring the survival and continuation of the organization.

COVID-19 brought along challenges where the safety practitioner (COVID-19 Officer) had to learn, deal, develop, implement, operate and monitor systems to ensure not only legal compliance but a humane and respectful approach in dealing with the pandemic as it unfolds. As heroes are made on the battlefield some perish, some survive and have the courage to stand up and talk about their experiences, journey and lessons learned to aid, support, direct and encourage others in similar circumstances.

For the safety practitioner this book provides a first-hand encounter through the lens of a COVID-19 Officer reflecting the experiences, challenges, journey, lessons learned and solutions to turn an enormous challenge into a health and safety victory.

JAG Pearson Mining and Industry Risk Control. Trading as Business Risk Management

If you are concerned about how your organisation will respond to an unexpected "Black Swan" event such as the Covid-19 crisis or, closer to the skin, how such an experience may influence you at an emotional and spiritual level, you need to read this very personal and self-revealing introspection as seen through the eyes of one of South Africa's thought leaders in the intangibles of the safety profession, Andre Johnson.

Building capacity to create new knowledge rapidly, substituting rigid approaches and an outdated compliance mentality with dynamic and responsive structures, policies and processes when having to manage complex and ambiguous problems as introduced by the Covid-19 pandemic, can be overwhelming for the safety practitioner who have to spearhead his organisation's strategies and plans to overcome the severe, and often tragic consequences of such a pandemic, within the context of a conundrum of influences and obstacles typical to a complex society like South Africa.

This book is about dealing with the unexpected and is jam-packed with insights that challenges the conventional managerial wisdom, suitably balanced with razor sharp personal observations of the intangible nuances that the author, as a safety and health professional, frequently must face. The author's spiritual and intellectual journey is brilliantly shared against the unfolding of the Covid-19 pandemic and his metamorphosis from insensitive ignorance to becoming emotionally enlightened through his brave and unselfish dedication to challenge and overcome the fearsome reality and impact of the Covid-19 pandemic in his organisation, with the unwavering support of the relevant stakeholders and his family.

A must-read for health and safety practitioners who seldom take time to reflect on the intangibles of their profession and the enigma of excessive traumatic experiences throughout their careers, which is hardly ever recognised and, even worse, dealt with at a professional level.

Francois Smith, MSc Industrial Safety Management, University of Central Missouri, Member of the Advisory Council to the Institute for High Reliability Organising, California, USA.

An honest and thought provoking read that will add value to all risk professionals in dealing with an unexpected crisis. The 2020 lockdown will have impacted on everyone's lives and businesses. The mining industry during this time, was at the forefront of trying to navigate the ever-changing environment and Andre shares his experiences during this unprecedented time on the lessons learnt and opportunities for future planning and preparation. The pandemic has highlighted the fact that a crisis is best managed by proactive management and stakeholder engagement. His documented personal experiences during this period will benefit the reader in their own development as a Health and Safety Practitioner (Justin Hobday)

Mr Andre Johnson one of the most dynamic leaders in the Northern Cape Mining Industries. The book is immensely powerful and captures the aim of this journey. What I read so far, very captivating it summed up so many emotions felt over the past couple of months. What I love about the book is a confirmation of what I experienced when I met you the first time:

- *Passionate strong Leader*
- *Ethical*
- *Passionate about people no matter Level, Race or background*
- *Objective looking at the bigger picture*
- *Good Mentor in all scenarios*
- *Prepared to raise to any occasion*

I do also love the last chapter that indicates that life will always happen, but it is down to each of us on how to part take in the journey (Jo Marie Roselt).

Justin Hobday & Jo Marie Roselt

Sales and Marketing Director, NOSA (Pty) Ltd

Key Account Manager, NOSA (Pty) Ltd

FOREWORD

The events of 2020 will be etched in history for ever. Not since the Second World War, more than 80 years ago, has the world seen or experienced a global economic and social crisis to the proportions we have experienced. It is lockdown day 145 in SA. I am reading the chapters of Andre's work in my study where I have spent the majority of this lockdown... unlike Andre, who has in many ways been at the forefront of fighting this pandemic, caring about the health and safety of those who work with him day to day. Initially my conversation with Andre left me with a thought of how can he achieve this (the book) before his birthday? As I continue to work through this manuscript, I am more convinced that it is not about achieving a personal goal for Andre, but rather what he can and want to contribute through this book.

Johnson's primary contribution is not a single idea, but rather an entire body of work related to the Covid-19 pandemic. It has one gigantic advantage, nearly all of it will be essentially right. Johnson has an uncanny ability to develop and share insights about his work as a Health and Safety practitioner/ leader in the Mining sector.

As a business consultant for more than a quarter century, I have realised that business is chaotic and messy most of the time and that there is no perfect business story. This book is not an effort to create a perfect management handbook but rather Johnson's story and personal journey during the pandemic, often personal and religious views captured in the moment. Possibly an attempt to provide a cognitive and even moral map of how to deal with matters that impact people's lives and wellbeing.

In my own family we have discussed the concept of what difference would we like to make during the events of 2020. We simply phrased it "what is your lockdown legacy?". What would you like to achieve, or contribute during this time? John Quincy Adams will have understood Andre's lockdown message or legacy because he clearly understood what it was to be a leader when he stated "if your actions inspire others to dream more, learn more, do more and become more, you are a leader? Johnson is that leader – a leader who takes care of his people and stay focussed on the wellbeing of the organisation. Enjoy the read!

Niel Steinmann (Director) PEOPLE'S DYNAMIC DEVELOPMENT

M. Comm. Industrial Psychology (UP) • SMP (UP)

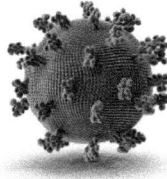

CHAPTER 1

PREFACE

On Sunday night, 15 March 2020, President Cyril Ramaphosa announced a "new normal" for South Africa (Notice, 2020b). This was exactly 10 days after South Africa's first Covid-19 case was reported and four days after the World Health Organisation (WHO) declared the virus a pandemic. I knew things would never be the same again. Among the announcements made that night and the regulations which followed were the ban on travelling, the closure of schools and mines, and the restriction of which businesses could perform essential services. We were confined to our homes, travelling was stopped, our social lives ended abruptly, and the workplace changed forever. We were caught with our pants down. A further shock was the announcement of a "peak" (Consultants, 2020) that was on its way, with two in every 100 people expected to die.

As in any organisation, through my lens, I was aware that I needed to quickly identify the structural weaknesses and threats to my organisation caused by Covid-19 which would affect consistent results. Simply stated, my objective was to keep the mine going despite the ethical responsibility I had during the health crisis.

This book addresses the situation where a high level of commitment is required to enhance and stimulate a social metaphor towards improving joint accountability to Covid-19 health and safety management. Aligning 3 800 employees to our Covid-19 procedures in less than four months requires a high level of trust, participation, and commitment (Johnson, 2018d). A Covid-19 Committee was thus created at the mine with the purpose of establishing an integrative resolution by considering opposing views, tensions, and valued perspectives (Johnson, 2018a). The results of the facilitation sessions, roadshows and leadership were an improvement in the health partnership, collaboration, and accountability towards the changes.

In addition, some autonomous units had a historical culture of fear and disrespected the health and safety rules at the mine. Therefore, the health and safety practioner requires a high level of integrative thinking, metacognition, self-awareness, empathetic skills, creativity, and the ability to leverage tensions to unpack and address the beliefs, misperceptions, and philosophies about this pandemic (Johnson, 2018a). Information, on the spread of the virus in South

Africa, from governmental departments and other sources was coming in rapidly and the health and safety operations needed to respond to these stimuli.

Such messy and complex problems as introduced by the Covid-19 pandemic come with different perspectives from multiple stakeholders which should be considered. The stakeholders present a pluralism approach as they do not share the same beliefs and values (Johnson, 2018d). Thus, a high level of mindfulness towards their various perspectives is required as no one sees the problem in the same way.

Furthermore, because of the Covid-19 regulations and my responsibilities at the mine, I was appointed as the Covid-19 Officer. In terms of Regulation 16(6)(a) of the Disaster Management Act regulations published in terms of Section 27(2) of the Act, "it was my duty to assist the Employer in ensuring compliance with the Act on the mine" (Johnson, 2020). Besides implementing the system, the last five months resulted in me having a higher awareness regarding my own consciousness from a level of dissonance associated with fear and anxiety to trusting my intuition (unconscious competence) to conscious competence as I developed my own emotional, intellectual and spiritual intelligence regarding this Covid-19 crisis (Johnson, 2017b).

The key questions on my mind through this journey were:

- What mechanism is required to implement the Covid-19 strategy and achieve alignment between the key stakeholders?

- Will the mechanism be related to my beliefs and will it improve the tangible and intangible benefits among the critical stakeholders during the Covid-19 crisis?

- Can the health and safety practioner learn anything from the journey I experienced? Can my lived experience of this crisis impact them and assist them with managing the tangibles and intangibles of future crises?

Through an outcomes-based action, the book addresses a need for leaders, employees, unions and middle managers to value health and safety and display commitment to the respect of human life and dignity by creating a partnership whereby compliance to Covid-19 regulations can be improved. This is to be supported by empathy, empowerment and a commitment to health and safety excellence with leaders at the pinnacle of the transformation (Johnson, 2018d). Furthermore, senior management and executives must be actively involved in the health and safety system, spearheading the dialogue, and visibly demonstrating commitment to the workers and the cause. Also, the employees should actively participate in health and safety by raising their concerns and expecting timeous feedback on the issues raised. We must value health and safety and change our paradigm to become a health and safety production process.

This transformation integrated the common values of joint accountability, trust, and conversations with action towards a shared value of proactive health and safety practices. Health and safety strategic conversations should involve an integrated approach, considering the context, mechanism, and outcome through a continuous feedback loop to enhance organisational mood, trust, and collaboration (Johnson, 2018b).

Also, the health and safety practioner requires a high level of mindfulness, emotional intelligence, ethical behaviour, integrative thinking, and metacognition despite his or her formal training. All of this is considered in this book, with each chapter focusing on a specific issue related to the Covid-19 crisis.

Chapter 1 addresses the Covid-19 context and subsequent sequence of events in South Africa since the lockdown was first announced on 15 March 2020. The management of Covid-19 does not merely require compliance with the regulations, it also requires a value-based approach which is the highest level on the health and safety maturity curve. To convert the beliefs and values in a four-month period presented challenges. It required a dialogue to address the beliefs and get alignment.

Tough, sometimes uncomfortable conversations regarding leadership philosophies had to take place to challenge the paradigms and assumptions during this time. The tension among the unions, workers and leaders were critical to move forward with our system implementation. The level of success of the innovation required diverse lenses to view the problem; it required a high level of metacognition and self-awareness when dealing with a complex problem like this. This level of thinking can integrate, categorise, abduct, and add purpose to the crisis. The integrative Covid-19 health and safety practioner reconciles the fragmented information to create a coherent whole.

Chapter 2 emphasises the implementation challenges and ideas as viewed through the ladder of inference through multiple perspectives. In South Africa's multicultural environment, you need to learn to listen, think and then respond. Also, our historical foundations determine the actions and decisions taken during a crisis and affect the assumptions we make and the meaning we assign to a specific situation. And the strategic approach you take to solving the problems at hand requires a leadership style that engages the people to form a shared value and alignment on the way forward. To improve the knowledge and direction of the system, we need to establish the conversation mechanism for coordinated action (Johnson, 2018b). Through the multiple perspectives, we can create a common understanding of the system to integrate the various viewpoints towards the development and expected outcomes of the system. This includes the tensions and conflicting views presented by many. Leveraging the tensions involves admitting our vulnerabilities and weaknesses. It thus requires courage to give feedback on the tensions identified as well as time and effort and a commitment to trust that the process will produce the required outcome. Authenticity increases this trust, cooperation, and commitment to the goal.

Chapter 3 follows the approach of obtaining the alignment by using a strategic in action approach. The mine consists of diverse generations, multicultural employees, and multiple contractors, and is a joint ownership mining company (Johnson, 2017a). The operations consist of three autonomous and yet interdependent units, each with its own leaders, organisational moods, cultures, and management styles. This chapter thus aims to align all the units in a limited period and calls for massive action to implement Covid-19 measures. In addition, the chapter considers the external environment in the form of the political, economic, social, technological, legal, and environmental (PESTLE) framework. So, balancing these perspectives and moving forward required massive integrated action to achieve the goals of business continuity during these turbulent times.

Chapter 4 investigates the support given to the critical production employees through a lens of Viable Systems Modelling (VSM) to ensure business continuity (Johnson, 2017a). It also considers the plans for certain "what if" scenarios as the infections are expected to increase. Four areas of concern were identified as contributors to the continuity of the mine, should the mine experience a partial or full shutdown due to the Covid-19 virus. A shutdown of the mine could be in the form of a partial closure of certain sections or the full closure of the mine due to employees being placed in quarantine or in isolation due to the expected outbreak. Here, I had to sharpen my own skills by completing an online course through the John Hopkins University to improve my own understanding of contact tracing and incubation periods caused by Covid-19 in order to educate the organisation on these issues. For the operations to be effective and sustainable, System 3 (S3) (management coordination) coordinates and integrates the System 1 (S1) (operations) function. System 4 (S4) is the planning and implementation role (Covid-19 Officer) and interacts with System 5 (S5) (top management and corporate). The purpose of this chapter is to improve synergy through improved coordination of the services and production departments to improve consistency in the production results.

Chapter 5 was written during the first three weeks of infections being diagnosed at the mine. It thus looks at the emotional experiences we went through as health and safety practioners, including my own perspectives when dealing with the other critical stakeholders during this time. This pandemic shows our true commitment and values. Those who are heroes in our society, in our communities and in our mines will show up during the crisis. It is the pinnacle of health and safety leadership. The crisis calls upon us to be role models and lead when people are depressed. We must look for opportunities to show optimism when people are the most pessimistic. Optimism eventually controls pessimism as it creates hope for a better future. This chapter's main purpose is to illustrate how to move from fear and inaction to empowerment and alignment.

Chapter 6 is a conversation directed towards Covid-19 Compliance Officers, Employees and Verifiers regarding clarification of the tangibles and intangibles. It also provides an overview of what has been done and clarifies key concepts during the implementation as viewed through my lens.

Chapter 7 concludes the book with a look at why I am writing this book as a Covid-19 Officer. During this time of crisis, I also lost my sister to cancer and I will soon celebrate a milestone birthday. So, this book is an especially emotional reflection for me. I am human after all and I have certain shortcomings, life experiences and beliefs which shape the decisions I make. This chapter also looks at my own self-development from dissonance to conscious competence during this period.

In conclusion, Covid-19 or a similar crisis will be around for many years to come. It is our "new normal" as our Human Resources Manager defines it. Yet, as an organisation, we have a new social and ethical responsibility towards the community and our employees. South Africa is a highly unequal society and a crisis like this has a major impact on the vulnerable and the poor. Most companies during this time have lost significant market capitalisation. Maintaining our social licence to operate converts into a different paradigm of maintaining our social and relationship capital in the future.

Considering the context of Covid-19 and the recent increase in Covid-19 infections in South Africa and the mine specifically, this book addresses the need to invest in the intangibles of the health and safety practioner. We need to address the adoption of proactive health and safety practices to improve the current situation of health and safety, not only at the mines, but also in the surrounding communities. As Covid-19 Officer, I can state that healthy and safe proactive mechanisms can be achieved by integrating the leaders and workers by aligning them to a common strategy.

Health and safety risk practices must be planned and monitored and require a level of joint accountability by ensuring the correct stakeholders are aligned to a shared value. The success of health and safety programmes will not only result in a reduction in fatalities, but also an increase in the connectedness and intangible transactions by providing a safety partnership based on values of care and collaboration towards a common objective of health and safe production.

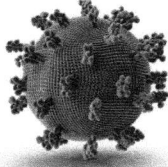

CHAPTER 2

IMPLEMENTATION
CHALLENGES

Introduction

The South African lockdown has been extended and, to many, this was not particularly good news. Under difficult circumstances, we remain obedient as it is for our benefit as well as for the benefit of our neighbour.

Interprovincial and inter district travel is still not allowed under the regulations of the extended lockdown. Yet, over the last two months as Covid-19 Officer, a legal appointment which three months ago I requested not receiving due to the potential conflicts I anticipated in the team, I have received many requests for personal travel which I then had to turn down. I spent three months in Africa in the early

2000s without any social life or family; it is a tough place to be. I empathise with those who have been away from their families since March 2020 due to the lockdown. I understand when they request to go home, but I had to turn down the requests. As the company appointed Covid-19 Officer, I cannot be seen to condone noncompliance. Do people realise the effect of their requests? I would knowingly be sending people to Covid-19 hotspots where they might possibly contract the disease. In addition, the requests are in violation of and contradicts the current legislation, even though political parties are currently contesting the constitutionality of the regulations as well as the contradictions among the various pieces of legislation.

But let us first define a "hotspot" (under Stage 3 of the lockdown) from our lawyer's viewpoint:

A "hotspot" means a geographical area or cluster of geographical areas.

"The regulations go further to list the following as hotspots:

Metros:

1. *Tshwane*
2. *Johannesburg*
3. *Ekurhuleni*
4. *Ethekwini*
5. *Nelson Mandela Bay*

6. *Buffalo City*

7. *Cape Town*

Districts:

1. *West Coast, Overberg, and Cape Winelands District Municipalities*

2. *Chris Hani District (Eastern Cape)*

3. *Lembe District (KwaZulu Natal)*

The regulations place the duty for the identification of hotspots on the Minister of Health. The identified hotspots must be Gazetted. In determining a hotspot, the Minister must consider the following criteria as a whole:

1. *Number of active cases per 100 000*

2. *Rate of increase of active cases*

3. *Availability of hospital beds and related resources*

4. *Any other factor, at the minister's discretion"*

At work, my Outlook calendar was pre-planned to address and prepare me for the upcoming Covid-19 committee meeting on the Friday before the long weekend of June 16 Youth Day. After all the work we have done since March 2020, why are we having this meeting, I wondered. Was there any relation between this unexpected "interprovincial travelling arrangements meeting" and the long weekend? Does this explain the WhatsApp messages I received two nights before regarding my role and power as Covid-19 Officer?

The meeting commenced with the clear context of relaxing the travel ban restrictions and ring-fencing certain people for personal travel. My assumption was correct regarding the meeting's intent and the WhatsApp messages I had received. Now is the time, I thought, that I need to voice my opinion and protect all the work my team did to protect the company. I must speak up, whether it is career limiting or not, I thought.

I started by saying, "I request the opportunity to speak freely", and then raised the following:

SMS/WhatsApp messages sent at 22:00 on Tuesday evening, informing me that I am overstepping my authority as Covid-19 Officer.

My private time with my family is being disrespected by messages late at night, causing me to lose sleep and peace of mind.

I feel that, as Covid-19 Officer, I am forced to support decisions which are against legislation and the Alert Level 3 regulations of the lockdown.

I am extremely uncomfortable signing any document which contravenes any of the Disaster Management Act regulations.

I have an ethical obligation to protect the employees of Mine.

In addition, the mine is the flagship for the bigger company and has been contributing more than 80% of the company's revenue over the last couple of years. Many executives and investors would be disappointed by our actions as leaders.

There were other biases in the room in support of personal travel. For example, the person taking the notes was biased, as reflected in the original notes of the meeting. These minutes I personally challenged, and the minutes were revised to reflect and express my views.

We are sometimes challenged as leaders on our authenticity which reflects our values. It reflects the decisions we make and the things we do and say.

When we agree with our values, we feel alive and in touch with ourselves. I am reminded here of a word we received in church recently: "Jesus lives in us. However, the evidence of His life must be seen. We have two responsibilities – let us see Jesus in those the Lord has given to lead us as well as in our neighbours and our children, our husbands, and wives. He is alive within them. To do so, we need to look without judgement so that we do not only see their problems and their mistakes. God and Jesus look at us differently. When God forgives us, He forgets our mistakes. What do you and I see in each other? We want to see Jesus. This is our responsibility. Our other responsibility is to make Jesus more visible in ourselves. Jesus must not be hidden in us but rather let Him be seen in us. This means we allow His nature to surface and be expressed in our thoughts, words, and deeds so that others can say, 'indeed, Jesus lives'."

We still have lots of work to do to grow in this context.

In chapter 1, I referred to the foundation, the rock. Our leadership style is one of stability and security. If you want to change something, you create enemies. People do not like change; more specifically, they want things to stay the same. They prefer their comfort zone in life. They say lessons will be repeated until they are learnt. If you decide to change something, for example if you want to lose weight, people look at you as if you are different. They look at you as if your commitment will not last. Sometimes you must end relationships if you want to grow or change. Covid-19 does not allow you to decide if change is an option, otherwise it will eradicate you. A health and safety practitioner's job are difficult. If you do good, you are criticised. If you do nothing, you are also criticised. So, rather do something good and get some personal reward out of it.

Regarding my team's commitment and perseverance, a large number of initiatives and Department of Health requirements have been put in place and the health and safety team has put in a lot of effort into the procedures, processes and documents created as per the legislative requirements. Some of us have been working every weekend since the lockdown started; others have been enjoying the family time, shifting the responsibility to the "willing" donkeys.

I do acknowledge that, as time progresses and the alert levels change, procedures might need to be revised to ensure accuracy and alignment with the practical application at the mine. However, I must uphold the law. I have a moral duty to uphold the law.

Even the current Covid-19 legal framework is conflicting due to the view of constitutionality expressed on social media. So, in conclusion, I do not support the notion of private travel, specifically before the peak, as it contradicts the legislation. Should my decision be overruled, I suggest that we revise the current travel form to a Travel Risk Movement form so that I can manage the Covid-19 risk upon return from hotspots. By the way, business travel is allowed. If you use the word "NO" lightly, the organisation will not move. So, only say "NO" to violations of legal and ethical issues. There is no such thing as a bad decision, but, if you have a compelling argument, I will change my opinion.

Reflection

When you become a leader, you no longer do the things you were once good at. The biggest challenge is changing from a manager to a leader. When you are a leader, people read everything you say or do. So, be consistent and repeat yourself.

Also, in South Africa's multicultural environment, learn to listen, think, and then respond. South Africa is in a leadership crisis. Our economy is crumbling due to the bad decisions the leaders made.

South Africa requires leaders to stop and think about their context. So, spend a significant time listening, without being judgemental. Ask why five times.

Our values decide how we will behave; our behaviour tells us what our values are. To transform ourselves requires narrowing the gap between who we are and who we think we are. This is part of being human. Our own thinking tells us a story about ourselves: whether we are good or bad. First find out who you are.

Yet, according to Schein (2004), *"culture is both a dynamic phenomenon that surrounds us at all times, being constantly enacted and created by our interactions with others and shaped by leadership behaviour, and a set of structures, routines, rules, and norms that guide and constrain our behaviour"*. We may not know what actions or intangible reactions are necessary regarding certain storms in our lives. Personal storms, such as the conflict situation above, require you to act as a health and safety practitioner. If we know what we want to do, we need to analyse and make sense of the problem by incorporating the perspectives of many to obtain an informed perspective. Any action will produce a reaction and so you need to be able to assess the consequences of your decisions from the context as it might impact the future of your organisation and your team. Your decisions result in one of two things: good consequences or bad consequences.

Good decisions are based on critical questions, affecting the greater good or big picture thinking. In ethics, it is defined as utilitarianism (Davis, 2018). It means choosing one action over other actions. Actions and decisions are based on our beliefs and assumptions due to our thoughts and ultimately our value system. For example, we all go through crises in our lives. Some big and others small. The issue in life is not these crises, but the foundation, the rock discussed in Chapter 1. A crisis only **exposes** your beliefs and the foundation of what you were built on. Your beliefs are more important than a crisis.

Times like these cause leadership philosophies to be questioned. How do we show up? Are we involved? People are watching and waiting to judge our authenticity regarding the company's values that we are preaching.

Whatever the strategic approach you take to solving the problems at hand, it requires a leadership style that engages people to form a shared value and alignment on the way forward (Johnson, 2018b). Historically, strategic health and safety systems were based on limited data analysis and interpretation. Perspectives were one sided based on the experience of the practitioner or, in some cases, the head office did the thinking for the people. Once the practitioner left, the system fell apart as it was based on that practitioner's limited beliefs. Some processes last, some do not.

Creating a shared purpose directs us what to go for. It adds meaning and drives everyone to the same goal. Tensions and barriers will come and go, but beliefs will remain (Johnson, 2018a). So, believe in zero harm, making a difference and assisting others to fulfil their purpose. Consider the graph in

Figure 1 on the injury reductions over a six-year period based on our belief in zero harm.

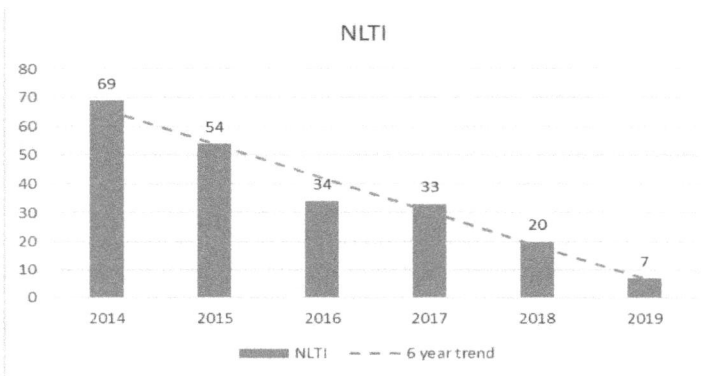

Figure 1: Non-Loss Time Injuries over a six-year period

Clearly, your belief system has a direct impact on your attitude and selfconfidence and ultimately the result. Romans 12:2 reads, "And do not be conformed to this world, but be transformed by the renewing of your mind, that you may prove what is good and acceptable and perfect will of GOD". Small daily wins create the emotional impact that allows you to amplify your attitude towards the expected outcomes (Schuh and Rhatigan, 2003).

If I need to consult and collaborate with more subject matter experts to get to the intended outcome, so be it. It develops self-confidence and keeps me going. The Covid-19 pandemic is only a crisis if you believe it is. If you believe it will penetrate our systems and affect 3 800 people, then it will. If, however, you believe that the impact will be impenetrable and will only affect a few, the outcome and focus will be different. Our beliefs determine the quality of the Covid-19 system that you will implement. You must change your perspective of the storm.

Yet, the reality is that Covid-19 has significant power and influence. It influences people with power, from the CEO to the Union Representative. Do you succumb to its power or do you have the right attitude to fight back? You must believe that if it does affect you, that you have the capacity to diagnose the impact and oppose its power. You can counter the impact of the crisis by developing counter forces to respond (i.e., a rebuttal). What is your response plan for the crisis (Model, 2014)? What are you expecting? What could happen? Thinking reflects your belief system.

The Johari Window (Figure 2) assists us to better understand ourselves and others. The Covid-19 crisis has revealed the Johari Window as it has revealed a lot of our own internal emotional battles. It has revealed our beliefs and how far we would go to act. The various conflicts, Covid-19 debates and information overflow have revealed the blind spots. Even those with less power and influence were heard like never. The Union members were heard as they have never been. We had to take them into account. Generally, I am a left-brain introvert, but my thoughts were clearly heard by all. My beliefs, assumptions and actions came to the fore. I am usually slow at showing empathy and compassion, but the pressure from the pandemic revealed much more. So, even though the world sees the pandemic as a death sentence, I see it as an opportunity to know ourselves better and to learn about our intentions, our character and how far we would go for the company.

Johari Window

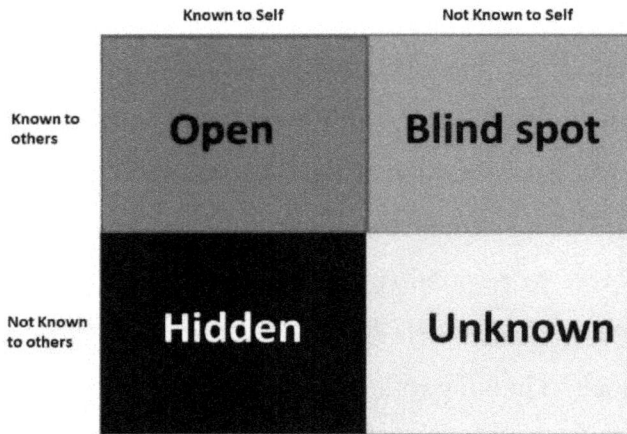

Figure 2: The Johari Window

It is time for spiritual reflection

Ephesians 3:16 reads, "That he would grant you, according to the riches of his glory, to be strengthened with might through his Spirit in the inner man". Many are suffering hardships during this Covid-19 period and this will persist for some time. We hope and pray that

God intervenes in this concerning time as soon as possible. We pray that God will strengthen our inner resolve with his Holy Spirit. The Holy Spirit cannot solve all problems, but it can strengthen us during this time.

Consider Jesus' temptation in the desert. When the devil decided to tempt Him in the desert, He overcame that temptation because of His love for and connection to His Father. His first source of strength was thus His love for His Father. Secondly, he trusted His Father so that He could fulfil His will and purpose in life. If we listen to the Holy Spirit, even if we do not know what is going on around us, we will be strengthened with wisdom. The third source of strength for Jesus was His knowledge and wisdom which started at a young age. The Holy spirit gives insight and inspiration. Jesus also had special wisdom; He knew when it was time to speak and when to keep silent. Sometimes, it is best to say we do not have all the answers. Our answer is that we believe in God and trust him. Do not waste your time with useless discussions; rather convince people with your actions and deeds. Jesus' last strength was His love for His neighbour. Even on the cross whilst He was suffering, He took care of Mary and John. He was able to forgive the people who killed Him out of love for His neighbour and God. These are just a few thoughts on how the Holy Spirit wants to strengthen us.

Development of the rich picture

As alluded to previously, to implement a system as complex as a Covid-19 system is not only dependant on the beliefs of the Covid-19 Officer. To expect a reliable outcome, the system must depend on the beliefs and expectations of those involved in the system.

Firstly, to improve the knowledge and direction of the system, we need to establish the conversation mechanism for coordinated action (Johnson, 2018b). Through multiple perspectives one can create a common understanding of the system to integrate the various viewpoints towards the development and expected outcomes of the system. This includes the tensions and conflicting views presented by many.

At the same time, learning can be achieved by all who understand the context of Covid-19 and develop meaningful courses of action. All people assign different meanings and make different assumptions of the system based on their values, life experiences and belief systems. The intent of the conversation design is coordinated and effective action towards the system development, as illustrated in Figure 3, and is triggered by the following questions (Strümpfer, 2017a):

- *"What is going on?*
- *What bugs you?*
- *What could happen?*

- *What should we do if...?*

- *What would you like?*

- *What must be done?"*

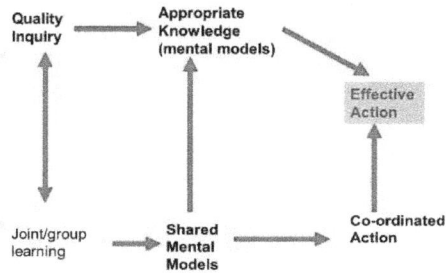

Figure 3: Coordinated and Effective action adopted from Strumpfer, 2016

The Covid-19 rich picture(Mann, 2004) best describes the situation and questions related to my concern expressed in Chapter 1 (Figure 4). *"How to diagnose the Covid-19 system's structural weaknesses and manage the intent on ensuring business continuity in anticipation of the storm?"*

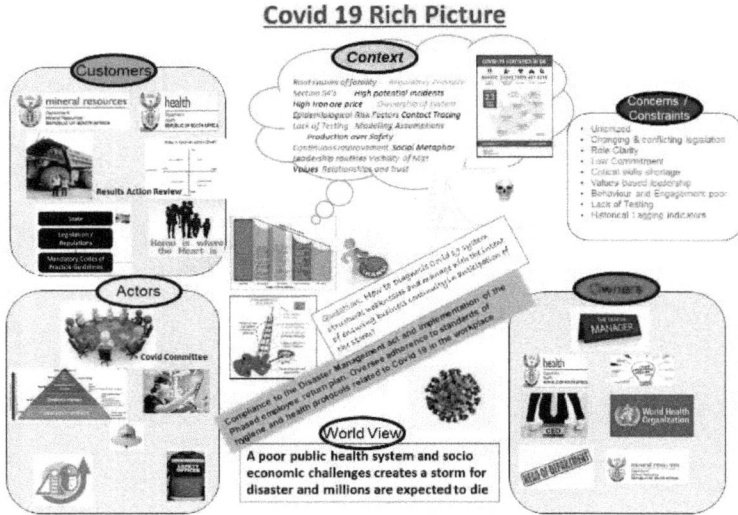

Figure 4: Covid 19 rich picture depicting the situation

From the above, many key stakeholders are involved, and I should anticipate a shared mental model of what ought to be and what ought to be done. Can we obtain a feasible and acceptable/representative mental model of desirable behaviour? A common belief is that the system can be improved by common coordinated action towards the question posed in the Covid-19 rich picture. Can we improve the historical low intangible transactions and take various people along with us on this journey? Intangible transactions in 2016 were as low as 20% (Allee, 2008). Is there an opportunity to improve this by knowing the context?

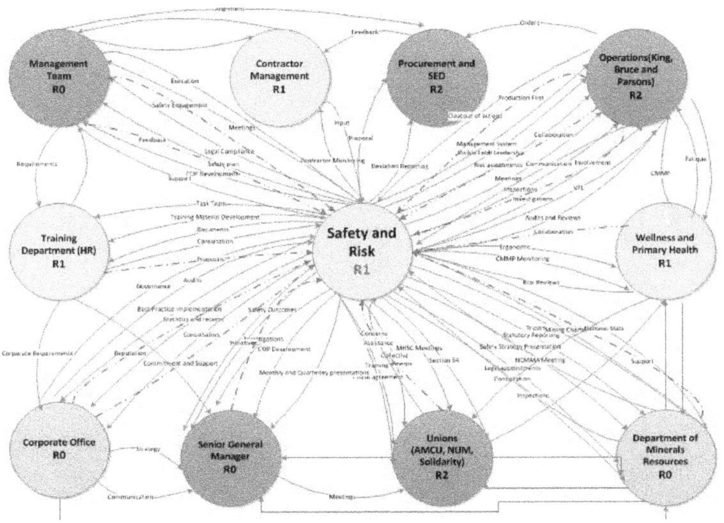

Figure 5: Illustration of the tangible and intangible transactions as viewed in 2016

Enhancements to the ladder of inference

Considering the above situation, the concerns and constraints related to intangible transactions, and the rich picture and belief systems, it is evident that a coordinated approach is required to address the Covid-19 system issue and ensure the appropriate change management approach is taken amidst the crisis. Better stated, the ladder of inference becomes (UCT, 2014): the intended outcome is high precision and high accuracy decision making and a shared value (Figure 6).

The Covid 19 Officer Ladder of Inference

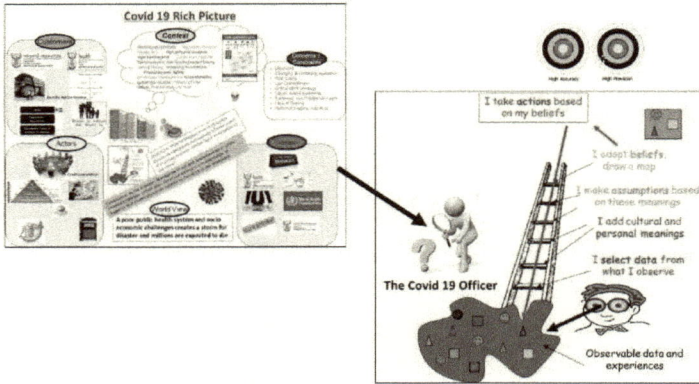

Figure 6: The Enhanced ladder of inference integrated with the rich picture

The Covid-19 Officer becomes the mediator between the views/perspectives of all in deriving an acceptable and representative mental model for coordinated action. The outcome from listening to the Actors (those involved), Customers (the beneficiaries of the system), and Owners (those with power to stop the system) and considering the question and constraints are shown below (Mann, 2004).

Considering the above, the Covid-19 Officer should be mindful of the impact of his own biases when making decisions and deciding on a course of action for the organisation. All these perspectives and critical focus areas were drawn from interactions during the last three months with various stakeholders (Figure 7). The perspectives from the PESTLE analysis discussed in Chapter 1 are also included.

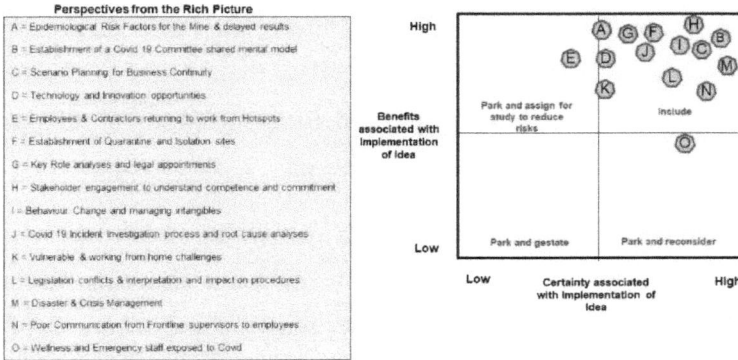

Perspectives from the Rich Picture

A = Epidemiological Risk Factors for the Mine & delayed results

B = Establishment of a Covid 19 Committee shared mental model

C = Scenario Planning for Business Continuity

D = Technology and Innovation opportunities

E = Employees & Contractors returning to work from Hotspots

F = Establishment of Quarantine and Isolation sites

G = Key Role analyses and legal appointments

H = Stakeholder engagement to understand competence and commitment

I = Behaviour Change and managing intangibles

J = Covid 19 Incident Investigation process and root cause analyses

K = Vulnerable & working from home challenges

L = Legislation conflicts & interpretation and impact on procedures

M = Disaster & Crisis Management

N = Poor Communication from Frontline supervisors to employees

O = Wellness and Emergency staff exposed to Covid

Figure 7: Illustration of the various coordinated perspectives for action

Final reflection on tensions from the ladder of inference

This chapter contributes to the mine by stimulating a social metaphor towards improving joint accountability for Covid-19 management, improving trust and participation to move the organisation into a higher level of safety maturity and aligning to the vision of zero harm caused by Covid-19 (Johnson, 2018d). This chapter assisted me in the development of my own integrative thinking capability which includes metacognition, improved selfawareness of my empathetic skills and creativity, and the ability to leverage tensions from many stakeholders (Johnson, 2018a).

The final reflection deals with my experience in the development of the rich picture and my integrative thinking capacity. During the Covid-19 committee sessions, I experimented with applying an empathetic approach in my relationships with the team members. The characteristics of an empathetic person relate to having compassion and entail doing good work and standing for ethical actions. Empathy and kindness are interrelated and demonstrate a commitment to helping others to achieve their goals or challenges. The outcome of the rich picture and focus points is an empathetic style towards health and safety partnering.

Metacognitive thinking together with an ongoing meditation practice resulted in a greater awareness of my own thinking (Johnson, 2018a). It provides clarity, relevance, purpose and meaning of your assumptions. It is a skill required for strategic thinking and could assist in creating effective outcomes. Metacognition together with pragmatism allow us to expand our limiting perspectives and create new direction and purpose (Feilzer, 2010). What used to be impossible now becomes possible.

My reflection on creativity included the selection of diverse team members with diverse brain profiles and enneagrams to develop creative solutions.

Finally, during the process, certain tensions arose. The ability to leverage the tensions is a unique skill required to place the difficult issues to be resolved on the table (Johnson, 2018a). Leveraging the tensions includes admitting our vulnerabilities and weaknesses. It, therefore, requires courage to give feedback on the tensions identified. It allows for giving time and effort and a commitment to trust that the process will produce the outcome. Authenticity increases trust, cooperation, and commitment to the goal.

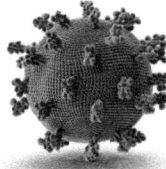

CHAPTER 3

ACHIEVING STRATEGIC ALIGNMENT

Context

The day after President Cyril Ramaphosa further lifted Level 3 lockdown restrictions, I received a message from Rebecca one of the Safety and Health Officers at the mine. *"Mr Johnson, I would like to see you for a couple of minutes."* *I paused and wondered what this could be about as I had a personal appointment after 16:00 that day. Rebecca said, "Thank you for your leadership style. If you want to see the type of leader that you are, I think the best way would be to look at all your departments. Look at the good things that are happening. Look at your achievements. I want to commend you for what you have done. I am just a Safety Officer. People might not like the type of leadership style you have. Others might like it. If you are*

45

genuine and you know who you are, people can smell it. To show humility like you have during this difficult time is hard. To ask forgiveness for the times that you hurt your staff in the last three to four years is hard. But you did it. You asked everyone to pull through during this difficult time of Covid-19, and we all need to take out the best for what is coming. Anyway, that calls for character. People can smell it if you're genuine."

I responded, *"If you consider how they used to fight wars in the Roman times, the two armies would approach each other, and the one king would first meet the other king in the middle of the battlefield. Sometimes the two kings would fight personally, and the war would be over. Other times they would speak the last words to each other before the battle began. Leadership calls you to sometimes take the lead, show courage and face the enemy head on. Leadership also calls for humility. It is now more than 100 days since the first Covid-19 case was diagnosed in South Africa. The President of South Africa mentioned last night that the rate of active infections is now doubling every second day. During Level 4, he mentioned, it doubled every 14 days.*

What happened at the neighbouring mine, where 39 people tested positive, caused me to react by insisting that all gets screened daily coming from the ZFM municipality. I had to provide clarity to the situation as the area was now officially a Hotspot. On Monday, I gave an instruction to remove all the return to work stickers of about

400 employees. I had to get all to redo their primary screenings and submit their daily contact tracings and travel movement registers. Some were not happy with my response; some criticised it, while others appreciated it. But I can tell you for sure that, since Monday, we have managed to identify six additional people who could have potentially brought the virus into our gates through the screening."

The change brought about by the sudden Covid-19 crisis has reference. It is like our reference as Christians in John 14:6, which says, "I am the way, the truth, and the life. No one comes to the Father except through me". It assists Christians to have a reference or a baseline to work from, irrespective of the circumstances and challenges they must face.

As soon as we have made sense of the Covid-19 concern as depicted in the rich picture discussed in the previous chapter, we need to reference it to something. As a mine surveyor, which was my previous career in the early 2000s, I need a baseline or reference before I can survey anything on a property. So, before you can measure any volume or property, you first need a point of reference or baseline referenced to True North with exact coordinates and elevation. So too, regarding the Covid-19 change, before implementing a system to counter the impact of Covid-19, you need a reference.

Our reference is the Safety, Health and Risk base established between 2015 and 2020 (Figure 1). Our baseline has reference to our culture, our values, and the previously implemented system. Yes, this also had challenges in implementation, some of which still exists today. However, it gives us an orientation to work from.

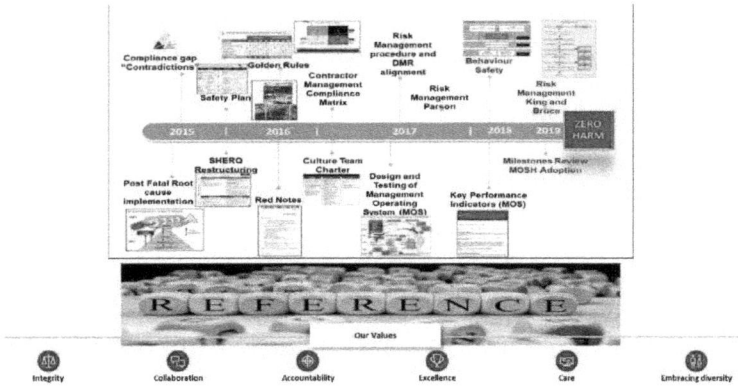

Figure 1: Previous Health and Safety Baseline regarding implementation status

From this base, we can establish how the current crisis affects us and how the baseline ultimately needs to be aligned to our current system. This base allows us to act and consolidate previous strategies to help us in our current crisis. It assists us in identifying what worked and what did not. This chapter seeks to translate the identified joint perspectives from the previous chapter and historically into action to improve the effectiveness of Covid-19 strategies and align it to the baseline already established at the mine.

The mine consists of diverse generations, multi-cultural employees, and multiple contractors, and is a joint ownership mining company (Johnson, 2018b). The operations consist of three autonomous and yet interdependent units, each with its own leaders, organisational mood, culture, and management style. This chapter also aims to align in a limited period and calls for massive action to implement Covid-19 measures.

My context is one of rapid changing forces and influences from environment factors in the form of political, economic, social, technological, legal, and environmental influences affecting the business. See the updated PESTLE from additional team input since the previous time and stimuli (Figure 2). This is our life; things happen, and we need to adapt. Our world is dynamic and ever changing. These inputs and changes to the PESTLE analysis were triggered by the 39 cases at the neighbouring mine and touched on our vulnerabilities as a mining community.

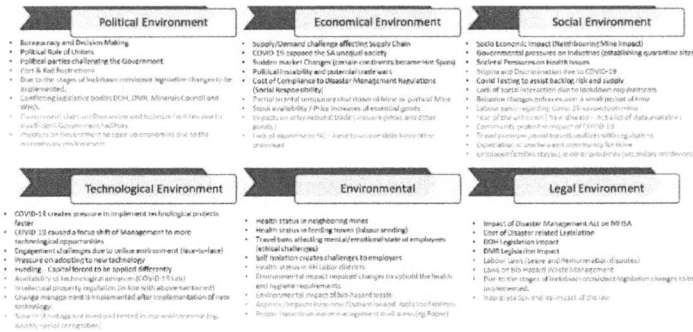

Figure 2: Updated PESTLE Analysis following multiple perspective inputs

Not responding suitably to the stimuli could hamper our growth and sustainability. The rich picture (Mann, 2004) in Chapter 2 posed a question: How should we diagnose the Covid-19 system's structural weaknesses and manage intangibles with the intent of ensuring business continuity in anticipation of the storm?

Early outcomes indicate that participation in the strategic process can be improved and requires an alignment through a performance management system among operations, corporate, top management, middle management, Unions, employees, and contractors concerning the strategic direction and priorities. Participation and alignment can be improved through the development of a conversation framework whereby assumptions are unearthed, and alignment of the opportunities and small wins (Schuh and Rhatigan, 2003) are aligned to create business continuity, even if impacted by the storm.

The approach also highlights a need to develop resource and strategic capabilities so that efforts can be coordinated and directed to the strategic narrative of the organisation (Johnson, 2018b). Strategic conversations should maintain an integrated approach, considering the Context, Mechanism and Outcome (CMO) through a continuous feedback (Strümpfer, 2017b) loop to enhance organisational mood, trust, and collaboration (Denning, 2012).

Our beliefs and the mental models we hold of a given situation underpin our actions (UCT, 2014). An appropriate coordinated action can be achieved by generating a shared mental model which can only be achieved through effective conversations (Johnson,

2018b). This principle leads to joint learning, strategic alignment, and action.

The strategy process allows for the planning of an approach by addressing the purpose of the planning process, increasing the knowledge of what needs to be done and enhancing the quality of decision making. It also allows a double loop learning (Strümpfer, 2018), as it changes beliefs, assumptions and mental models through effective conversation and inquiry, thereby creating a shared mental model of the future on which to act on (rich picture). For effective results or outcomes to be achieved, the process needs high levels of quality and must be accepted by all (Results = Quality x Acceptance).

Illustration of the strategic approach

The conceptual model of the strategy in practice developed below was based on my theory of how a strategy should be practiced. This is illustrated and is developed and refined by using strategic tools from the University of Cape Town and the Minerals Council of South Africa (Figure 3).

The historical context of my work environment situation is as follows:

- We tend to procrastinate, complicate issues, and lack the necessary action to succeed.

□ There is a lack of consistent, integrated, and continual action towards goals, and actions often lack the necessary momentum.

□ We have exceptionally good ideas in design but lack the momentum to see the idea or project to completion (Johnson, 2018b).

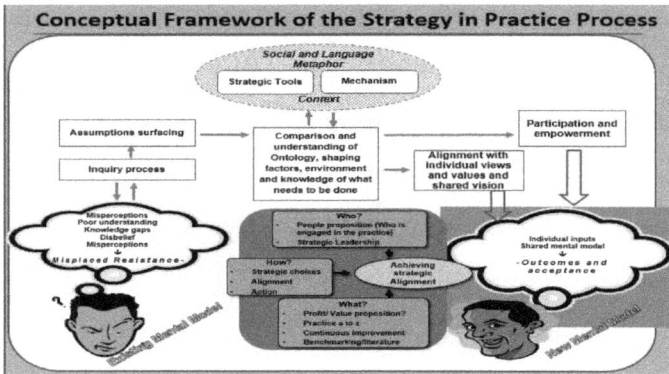

Figure 3: Conceptual Model of Strategy in Practice adopted from Strategy in Practice model, 2018

The situation is further complicated by organisational moods and emotions. Emotions are short lived and originate from a known cause; moods are feelings that are longer lasting (Denning, 2012). Organisational moods could be counterproductive to the strategic alignment process. Denning (2012) indicates that "[t]he moods and emotions of the people around us, our partners, teams, and groups, strongly affect performances. Positive moods enhance performance;

negative moods detract and can render teams and groups dysfunctional."

Leaders need to possess a high level of emotional intelligence to manage the moods and emotions in the organisation (George, 2000). This creates the misplaced resistance referred to in the model, which causes poor understanding, disbelief and misperceptions concerning the strategic alignment. Therefore, this model suggests that misalignment can be created if assumptions are not tested and surfaced through an inquiry process. To get things done, we need an emotional connection and a collective psychological contract.

Denning (2012) adds, "For collaboration to work, the group members need moods of appreciation, trust, and mutual commitment to the mission". So, teams that are good at collaboration are more likely to achieve their goals. Hence, a process of inquiry creates self-development and expansive learning takes place through participation and the resistance to challenge the ladder of inference of the team or individual.

To achieve strategic alignment and a common value of the shared vision, the strategic alignment process follows a series of conversations (Strumpfer, 2017). A strategy is not about the selection and application of a strategic tool, but rather a process of considering an end view by creating organisations that survive, thrive, and develop new approaches to remain viable. It focusses on why we should take certain actions and what should we be doing in each situation.

The inquiry process continues with getting an understanding of what is going on around us. What is our context? What are the key concerns we are facing? It then continues to develop possible future scenarios and a set of strategic responses to the ontology facing the organisation (Strümpfer, 2017a). Through conversations and adding meaning to the complexity, we can determine the objective ontology facing the organisation from the subjective multiple perspectives of the participants. The idea here is to get a common understanding of the ontology which are shaping environmental factors and create a knowledge base of what needs to be done (Johnson, 2018b).

Descriptive theory for Covid-19

There is expected that high commodity prices will not last due to the current shutdown of mines in South America. At least, that was the view prior to Covid-19. During 2015 and 2016, the company went through a difficult time with a downward cycle in commodity prices. Demand for the mineral is expected to decrease, while global supply will increase. Taking Covid-19 into account, the current supplies are being reduced due to certain parts of the globe experiencing a peak in infections and mines being shut down. Closer in South Africa, mines are issued with Section 54s, following Covid-19 cases.

To counter the effect of expected lower margins, the Covid-19 theory is best illustrated in the CMO illustrated in Figure 4 (Braun, 2002). This descriptive theory best describes the situation of concern and the mechanism to be adopted to achieve the challenges described in the previous chapters. We must also invest appropriately during this period in mechanisms not only to reduce the impact of the storm, but also to prepare the organisation for further potential waves, as seen globally.

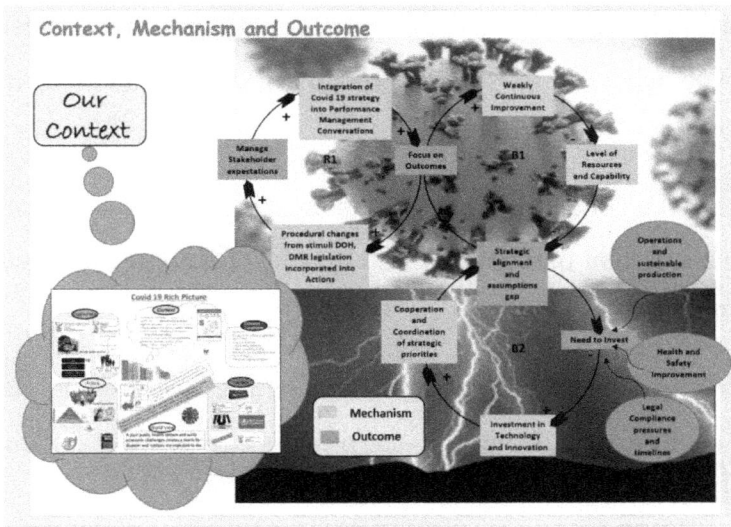

Figure 4: Context, Mechanism and Outcome for Strategic Covid Management in the future

Generally, there is a reluctance from mining companies to reinvest due to the high cost of compliance as well as environmental, legislative, and societal pressures within the South African context.

Covid-19 risks accelerated this decision to invest mainly from a Health and Safety perspective. Some decisions to obtain capital approval would historically be executed in two to three months. Clearly, a crisis creates a certain emotional and ethical response and leads to very quick approvals.

Yet, all must collaborate, and strategic alignment is needed. There are, however, a gap concerning strategic capability and resources as well as misalignment of strategic intent among the stakeholders. This type of archetype is referred to as a growth and underinvestment archetype, where there is a limit to future growth (Kim & Anderson, 1998).

For the given context, using a certain intervention and mechanism to produce a certain outcome, a strategy in action approach (Figure 5) is recommended (Jarzabkowski et al., 2016).

This is where the "WHO" needs to be identified (Strümpfer, 2017b). Who should participate in the process? Who are critical for execution? The specific organisational positions and characteristic traits will have implications, if not selected properly. "WHAT" practice should be applied to the organisation in the given context is just as important for effective strategy execution. Finally, "HOW" the action will be created from the selected strategic choices and implications for the transformation process should be identified. The outcome of the strategic process is dependent on the interaction and feedback between these three.

Strategy as practiced in the organization

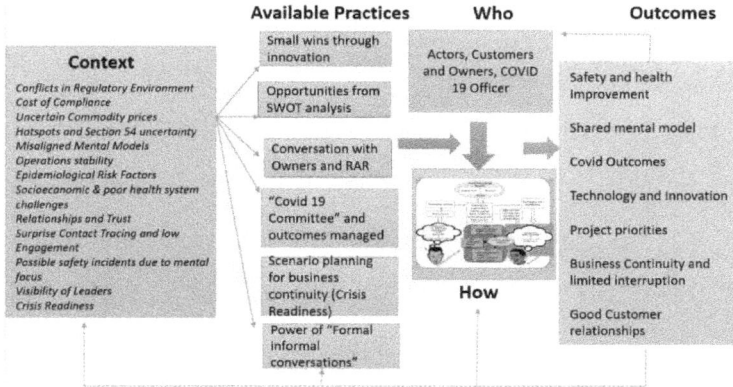

Jarzabkowski, P., Kaplan, S., Seidl, D. & Whittington, R. (2016). On the risk of studying practices in isolation:

Figure 5: A Model for strategy in practice adapted from Jarzabkowski et al., 2016

To summarise, strategy in practice results in you creating an ontology of the organisation and defining where you are. It requires you to be aware of your assumptions and the organisational assumptions, before attempting to change the organisation. An organisation is a system of conversations which allows you to create a narrative through a social system model of dialogue, where people create the future together through high trust and empowerment (Strümpfer, 2017a). The conversations should include monitoring actions (execution) through ongoing reflection. Strategy starts by asking yourself what mindset you would like to create based on your future ontological assumptions and then developing a framework to suite the context of the business and organisational mood.

Applied to Covid-19 technology and innovation

Prior to Covid-19, the SouthAfrican government discussed plans to accelerate the implementation of the Fourth Industrial Revolution. The unintended consequence of such massive implementation of technology is potential job losses. Due to the extended lockdown (now more than 100 days), more small businesses will be closing, there will be massive retrenchments and the lockdown will negatively affect economic growth. This leads to a double impact on jobs, with the impact of technology and the impact of Covid-19, which will only further exacerbate the already high unemployment situation in South Africa.

In the context of Covid-19 implementation, we should be considering the rebuttal to this debate (Davis, 2018). How can technology assist us in challenging this paradigm? How can we use technology to our advantage to mitigate the risks associated with Covid-19? As we prepared the business for a start-up and steady return to work, during the first 21 days of the lockdown, we came up with a concept of mass thermal screening like the processes used at airports. This was still during the time when people were in shock, the streets were empty and there was panic buying. Instead of going into shock, we had to come up with a different style of thinking. This paved the way for what was to come. We needed to mass scan 20 to 30 people simultaneously and, from this mass scanning, identify people with temperatures more than 37 degrees.

This sudden focus on digital technology provided an opportunity to adopt off the shelve innovation. As soon as you internalise this goal, it makes you more consciously aware and results in additional ideas and new opportunities for technological improvement being noticed. Clearly, if the mine wanted to survive, we needed to develop innovative strategies to assist in our preventative mechanism. If we could immediately identify people with a fever and high temperatures during the primary screening, we could significantly improve our position.

One of the critical stakeholders raised the question during the Covid-19 Committee meeting, "*Is Screening at the gate for high temperatures?*" Sometimes a simple question triggers a certain response. Clearly, we needed to reassure the stakeholders that the results using the obtained technology would be reliable.

So, the next step was to ensure that the system remains stable and accurate. By implementing basic critical checks through the development of critical tasks to be performed on the instrument and introducing a daily and weekly routine, we could be confident that the results would be reliable and accurate. This meant that we needed to set clear expectations regarding the focus of the frontline workers involved in this screening process to ensure the accuracy and reliability of the results (Figure 6). Never assume technology works; get processes in place to validate and verify.

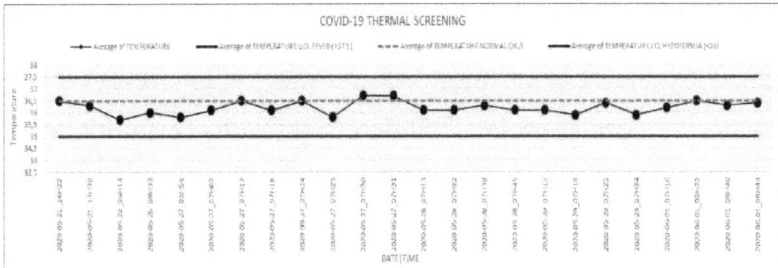

Figure 6: Control Chart to monitor variation

Leadership is required to optimise and integrate the Fourth Industrial Revolution so that it is not seen as a threat to job security, but rather an opportunity to mitigate the risks. The technological and innovative concept is summarised in Figure 7. The questions are focused on the innovative model to support and speed up the Covid-19 implementation model.

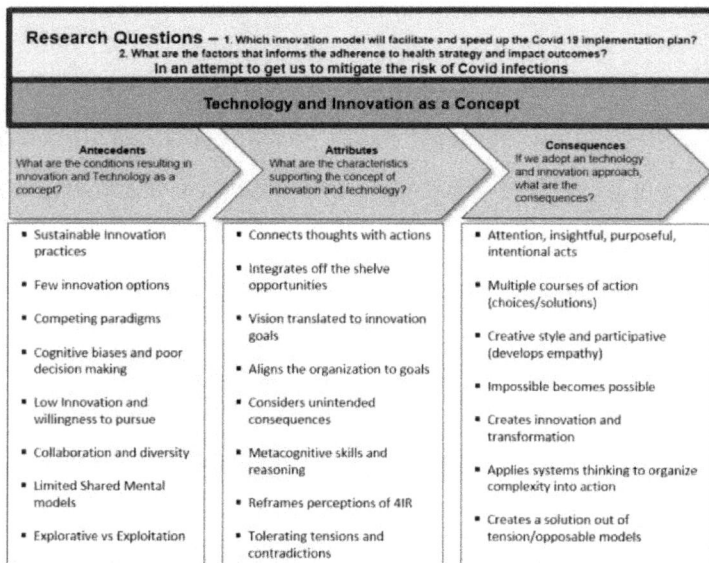

Figure 7: Technology as a Concept Analysis

From various brainstorming sessions, some quick wins were identified. These are listed below.

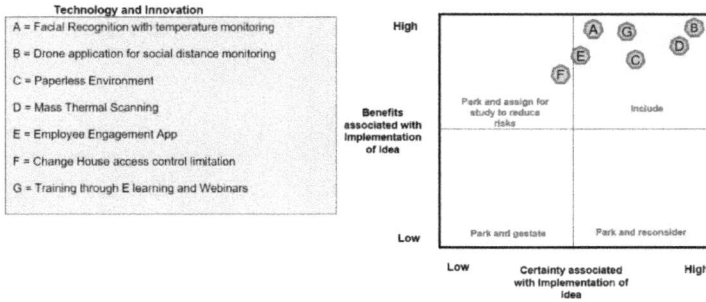

Figure 8: Some Strategic Covid 19 Innovation Ideas

Focussed outcomes through joint accountability

Asurvey (Johnson, 2018d) conducted during 2018, involving the perspectives of senior managers, engineers, and operators, revealed a certain level of commitment and competence towards health and safety illustrative of the culture in the organisation (Figure 9).

Commitment and Competence of our own employees?

Level	Commitment to Safety and Health			Safety & Health Management Competence		
	Low	Medium	High	Low	Medium	High
Senior Managers (HOD's)	5	22	13	7	23	10
Engineers/Managers	2	26	13	8	21	12
Supervisors and Foremen	9	24	9	11	23	6
Artisans	13	21	5	14	21	5
Operators	18	20	4	16	20	2
Trainees	7	11	4	6	12	1
Safety Team members	1	22	15	8	16	15

Figure 9: Safety Culture Survey conducted in 2018 showing commitment and competence of certain roles

The lower level of commitment illustrated by the amount of perspectives from the various employees interviewed was concerning. This is another tension related to our situation during the Covid-19 pandemic.

Figure 9 illustrates that the role of leadership in setting the culture for health and safety increases the level of commitment, trust and ultimately competence to the process. Leaders improve the commitment of those below them through their commitment and by providing the necessary support for the lower levels. To improve the commitment, as illustrated above, requires shared assumptions and visible leadership to aid conversations towards improving the state of our Covid-19 system.

Another assessment illustrates the balance of power in the mining industry inherently caused by the way legislation is prescribed in the Mine Health and Safety Act (Figure 10). The act places significant legal power on the CEO and employer compared to the lower levels of the organisation.

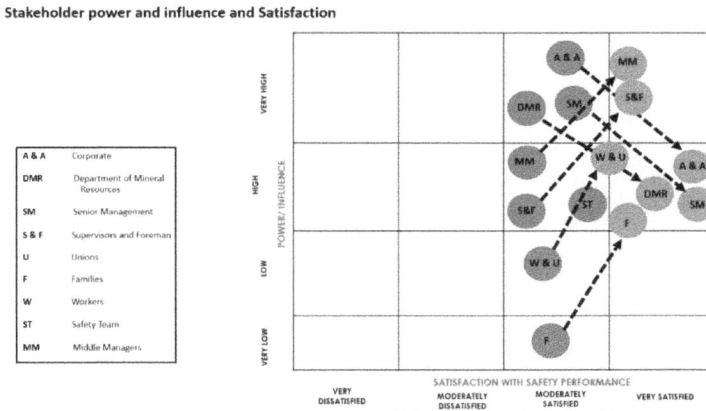

Figure 10: Safety Culture Survey conducted in 2018 illustrating power and influence regarding health and safety decisions

This level of power and influence placed on the managers could be a counter force to the lower levels' commitment, as illustrated in 10. Yet, in the context of Covid-19, a different approach is required. You expect people lower in the organisation to be empowered to make decisions and take the necessary actions. You expect a higher level of commitment and competence towards Covid-19. You expect management to "give up" their power as the masses are being exposed to Covid-19. This leads to a significantly different approach to "balancing the power" as mentioned by one of the Union members. This leads to the following questions:

- *How do we change the imbalance of power created historically by our legal appointment process?*

- *How can increasing the power at the lower levels increase the level of commitment as this is where the masses are?*

Firstly, regulations published during the Disaster Management Act call for the appointment of a Covid-19 Officer to oversee the implementation of the phased employee return plan and implement the relevant health risk controls to mitigate the spread of the virus. It is a massive task to consider 3 800 employees, while being mindful of the historical challenges faced regarding increasing the power of the lower levels and improving the level of commitment.

A perspective raised by one of the Union members was that the Covid-19 Officer is a management representative by nature and creates an imbalance of power. To address the issue and to ensure a process of joint accountability to the cause, a Covid-19 Committee was established (Figure 11).

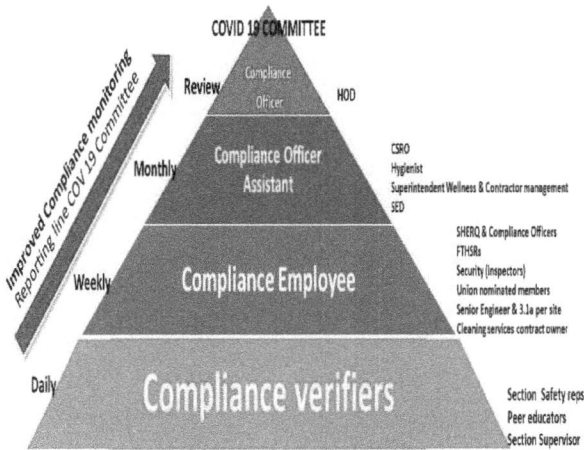

Figure 11: Legal Compliance process to balance the Power adopted from the outcome of the Covid-19 committee

The Committee meeting's agenda basically entailed the critical items to be addressed and implemented by the Covid-19 Officer. Additional levels, representing the employees, contractors, engineers, safety officers, hygienists, and other relevant stakeholders (some actors and some customers), as defined in the previous chapter, were identified (Lewis, 2017). These were first legally appointed as delegates to the Covid-19 Officer, and then trained and expected to perform certain Covid-19 legal inspections aligned to the recently published Code of Practice for Covid-19. The roles of the Covid-19 Officer's assistants are to assist in the implementation of the plan, covering health risk controls, as outlined in the procedures, COP and regulations. Compliance employees, besides monitoring social distancing, will also assist in ensuring that the employees adhere to directions and standards related to hygiene controls and the limitation of exposure to Covid-19. Compliance verifiers were appointed to monitor and verify operational controls.

The Committee will provide "continuous feedback and weekly actionbased meetings. This results in improved levels of trust and improved social networks as remarked by the key stakeholders. The Unions (Taylor, 2020) also support the process and the general feeling is that the mine is looking after the best interest of the employees" (SANS 16001 Feedback, 2020 audit).

Final spiritual thoughts

Ephesians 3:16 reads, "That He would grant you, according to the riches of His glory, to be strengthened with might through His Spirit in the inner man". Many are suffering hardships during this period. I pray that Our Heavenly Father intervenes and changes this situation. I pray that the Lord strengthens our inner man, our gifts, and our talents so that our wisdom can increase, and we can make the correct decisions to the benefit of all.

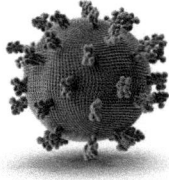

CHAPTER 4

BE PRAGMATIC WHEN ASSESSING YOUR CAPABILITY

Introduction

This chapter highlights that the mine needs to sustain its performance concerning the supply of a high-grade quality product to a niche market, despite Covid-19's impact. To achieve this high level of quality ore, volume of sufficient product quality is needed to sustain the mine's performance. A look at the impact of Covid-19 on the viability of the mine reveals that sufficient stockpile should be maintained if a business disruption occurs.

Four areas of concern were identified as contributors to the continuity of the mine, should the mine experience a partial or full shutdown due to the Covid-19 virus. These are:

1. The sustainability of the blasting contractor and the associated mining activities, which could result in low floor stocks.

2. The ineffective resource utilisation related to the absence of human resources caused by self-quarantines or self-isolations.

3. The low run of mine stockpiles, caused by the absence of critical contractors or associated activities further down the mining value chain, for example, the plant; and

4. The communication and feedback loops concerning key Covid-19 performance controls. Communication dispels fear and uncertainty. So, unclear communication from my office down to the lowest level regarding the testing of all employees potentially caused a strike.

Having identified these four areas of concern enables us to further identify weaknesses and threats in our organisation which affect consistent results (Johnson, 2017a). It also enables us to see if purpose and culture are present in the autonomous units to ensure the overall goal of the organisation is achieved.

I am also mindful of historical behavioural and communication issues identified during the previous health and safety interventions as well as those issues identified from our leadership behavioural diagnosis discussed in the previous chapter (Johnson, 2018a). These issues include:

▫ Identifying critical contractors getting infected and the critical roles or departments in the organisation, such as the backup teams for contractors as well as the wellness and emergency services crews should they become infected.

▫ Ring fencing critical revenue production processes; and

▫ Staggering and rotating shift configurations for continuity of the operation.

We should furthermore identify consistent Covid-19 standards and messaging across all three sites, considering the leadership practices and behaviours affecting the cultures of the autonomous units (Johnson, 2017a). All of this affects the level of business continuity and consistency. If not addressed, it could affect the sustainable delivery of the product in an environment of high commodity pricing. Although high pricing is short lived, the mine should rather use this economic benefit supported by better exchange rates as is currently the case.

It is time for spiritual reflection

John 4:9(a) reads, *"Then the woman of Samaria said to him, how is it that you, being a Jew, ask a drink from me?"* Among Jesus' many qualities was teaching. He was direct and did not exclude anyone. He approached the

Samaritan woman at the well; despite the spiritual diversity and cultural differences between Jews and Samaritans, there were also similarities, for example, both groups believed in the same God. He also associated with a Samaritan woman, who had a questionable history, and had a conversation with her. Moreover, he reached out to those on the fringes of society so that the gospel could be preached to all.

We are sometimes opinionated about certain people. This may be because they do not have the same social status as we do. We, however, miss the opportunity to empower them due to our prejudices and biases. We need to love those we meet for the first time; we should love those who feel ostracised. Let us fulfil our commission without any prejudice or judgement and remain unbiased. Let us understand our own context, including why we are here and what our purpose is.

Key focusing questions

In designing and diagnosing the actions to sustain the viability of the mine, five key questions will be posed upfront. These questions will assist me in creating a perspective of the situation, will help me identify relevance and will guide me in my approach (Johnson, 2017a). They are as follows:

1. How to use Viable Systems Modelling (VSM) to effectively diagnose the structural weaknesses of my organisation in a Covid-19 disaster situation (Espinosa and Porter, 2011)?

This question was selected to identify the areas causing possible production losses due to the unavailability of possible positive persons or persons under investigation (PUIs). It also determines whether the business plan expectations and key result areas will be achieved among the autonomous units in the case of a disruption. This question also determines whether consistency, purpose and culture are evident in the organisation and specifically in the three production units. Finally, it will establish if clarity regarding Covid-19 is made available to all the employees concerning the overall direction related to productivity and health.

2. How to identify threats to the organisation's viability and make suitable recommendations for improvement (Bates, Niles and Taylor, 2008)?

This question seeks to establish whether threats are present due to the changes in the Covid-19 environment and if suitable variety exists to respond to this complexity. It also seeks to identify gaps at the operation level which could become a potential threat if not managed or brought under control.

3. How to assess the effectiveness and information flow between System 3, System 4, and System 5 (Espinosa and Porter, 2011)?

For the operations to be effective, System 3 (S3) (management coordination) coordinates and integrates the System 1 (S1) (operations) function. System 4 (S4) is the planning and implementation role (Covid-19 Officer) and interacts with System 5 (S5) (top management and corporate). S4 also interacts with S3, S3* (health and safety audits) and System 2 (S2) based at the operations (Walker, 2001). S4 approves the Covid-19 communications and ensures the Covid-19 Committee gets the message and is aligned with the plan. Variety can be improved if the interaction between S3, S4 and S5 is regulated which can lead to improved empowerment of the operations (Walker, 2001).

This question considers whether the information systems and channels have been designed to deal with the complexity that it now faces. This highlights the gaps with the information flow from the environment to the operations and management and the organisation's response to these stimuli.

4. How to diagnose the role of System 3 in assessing the autonomy of my organisation?

S3, in its state, should always be directed towards the mission and objectives of the organisation. Management coordination is also responsible for optimising and ensuring synergy across the S1 primary value chain, if necessary, to ensure outputs are maintained (Walker, 2001). Are all the resources optimised in a state of business interruption to enhance synergy across the functions so that S1 reaches its objective to produce tonnes safely?

> *5. What are the other small wins from a mining and processing point of view to assist in the diagnosis of the organisation towards continuity?*

For communicationto be effective, we must be mindful of how communication flows in the organisation and how this assists the organisation in achieving its objectives.

(Walker, 2001), from work done by De Beer, compares the VSM to the way in which the human brain organises the operations of the muscles and organs to the effectiveness of an organisational model. He identifies six main functions interacting with each other for effectiveness:

1. **S1 (operation)** concerns who is responsible for producing. Put in another way, it looks at who is responsible for doing things, which justifies the existence of the entire system (Shelley, 2017) . This is compared with the muscles and organs in the human body. In the context of the organisation, this is the operation responsible for the primary production activities (Walker, 1991).

2. **S2 (stability/coordination)** performs a monitoring and coordination role. It is responsible for the coordination between the various sub-operational units. This could be related to a production plan where conflicts and disruptions are minimised to ensure smooth coordination between functions (Walker, 1991). In the human body, this would be the sympathetic nervous system. S2 provides a coordinating function, assisting S3 in its direction of the operations.

3. **S3 (synergy/integration)** is a task of senior management responsible for the day-to-day control and guidance of S1. The coordination role of S2 reports to S3, which is then responsible for the optimisation of the plan. Together with S3* and S4, it also ensures that variety from the environment is kept in homeostasis by responding to these perturbations. It performs a monitoring and coordination role, as it is responsible for the coordination between the various sub-operational units. S3 can be related to a production plan where conflicts and disruptions are optimised to ensure smooth coordination (synergy) between functions (Walker, 2001). In the human body, S3 is compared to the base brain which oversees the entire complex of the muscles and organs.

4. **S3* (auditing)** performs an auditing and monitoring function and interacts with S3 to maintain the operation's requisite variety. S3* could do this in the form of spot checks and Covid-19 audits (Walker, 2001).

5. **S4 (forward planning)** performs the intelligence function (Hilder, 2005). It contextualises the entire environment in which the operation finds itself and fulfils a future planning and forecast role. In the human body, this role is compared with the mid brain which, through the senses, makes a connection to the outside world (Walker, 2001). It also creates an understanding of the situation in which the organisation finds itself by interacting with S3. It concerns the functions of where the company is today and where it needs to be in the future (short-, mediumand long-term planning). It looks at the future events that may affect S3, for example, economic, education, commercial and technical factors.

6. **S5 (policy)** performs the overall policy making function (performance measures, management practices, and organisational design) in the organisation. S5 has ultimate authority and maintains the identity of the organisation. In the human body, S5 would be the cortex and higher brain functions (Flood and Jackson, 1991).

These six systems are essential to maintain viability in any operations.

In Figure 1, Beer sketches a basic diagram of a VSM, depicting its main elements as the operation, the meta system (or management) and the environment it interacts with (Walker, 2001). The VSM considers the study of an organisation and its environment and looks at the organisation's response to its environment. Within the environment, there is a process happening and, within the process, management is responsible for maintaining homeostasis.

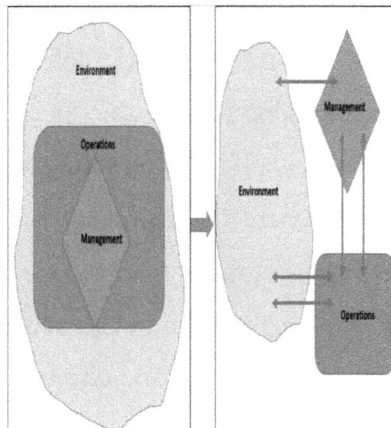

Figure 1: Basic Diagram of a Viable Systems Model adopted from Beer

The VSM diagram in Figure 2 illustrates the six sub-processes in the form of a VSM diagram adopted from (Walker, 2001). Here, the operations are depicted, with sub-processes along the value chain. This might be in the case of the mine, with the mining section responsible for blasting and hauling the ore and the process plant responsible for beneficiation. Each self-organisation also responds with its environment for resources, materials or energy and needs to remain viable within the bigger organisation of the mine.

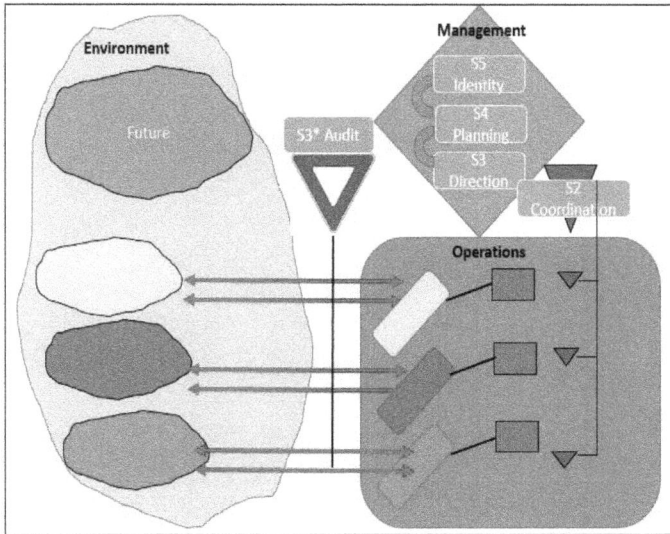

Figure 2: VSM illustrating the six processes

Identifying and clarifying the system and its purpose

The Covid-19 situation highlights where the mine needs to sustain its performance, concerning the supply of a quality product to a niche market, despite Covid-19 interruptions. The purpose of the organisation is, therefore, to optimally exploit the mineral resource to maintain shareholder wealth.

The production system defines the primary activities of the operational unit and whether they fulfil the mission statement of the organisation. The primary process might be mining in the value chain, but the sub-processes to achieve the mining process need to be defined for the operational unit to fulfil its purpose. Five core activities were defined to achieve the objective.

These are:

1. The mineral resource delineation and modelling.
2. The mining processes.
3. The metallurgical or beneficiation process.
4. The logistics (or transport) process; and
5. The final sales part referred to as marketing.

The mine has four operations, namely two mines, a processing plant, and the area where logistical transport takes place to the port.

The mines and the various subunits and departments have a high level of self-organisation in their approach towards the mine. Self-organisation here refers to a continuous process of reorganising to find the best fit with the environment and creating order from disorder (Bates, Niles and Taylor, 2008). Most of the team members realise the role the company plays, but the autonomy appears to be excessive with feedback and communication loops lacking in certain areas (Flood and Jackson, 1991). To maintain a consistent feed to the plant within a good product quality range, the two mines need to remain autonomous.

The mines are currently organised with a manager (S3) who is responsible for drilling and blasting and load and haul. The mines are continuous operations (24/7). The manager has S2 roles reporting to him and, in turn, reports to an S4 Head of Department Operations. In addition, there is a Breakdown and Maintenance Department, headed by the engineer, responsible for maintaining the fleet and assisting with breakdowns. The engineer reports to the manager mining. An additional line manager looks after the construction activities of roads and safety berms and the maintenance of haul roads in the mine.

In total, five critical contractors are employed at the mine. One is responsible for maintaining the primary and secondary roads. Another is responsible for blasting. A third is responsible for the supply and maintenance of drill bits and hammers, while another is responsible for topsoil stripping. The fifth contractor is responsible for the supply and maintenance of mobile toilets and kitchens.

The mine has been battling to maintain a consistent feed to the crusher as well as to achieve the waste stripping ratio. The role of S2 has mainly been to monitor quality control, the availability of equipment fleet and compliance to the maintenance schedule. In addition, S2 fulfils a coordinating role with a huge focus on planning and availability of resources. From an environmental point of view, various factors (perturbations) influence production (Walker, 2001). The mine must attain a high level of cooperation and coordination to remain successful.

The core function behind S2 is to maintain stability through effective coordination (Walker, 2001). This is achieved though the management of the operational activities through the execution of the short-term plan. A key input into the short-term plan is the availability of blocks for blasting, sufficient floor stocks of suitable quality for the loading and hauling destination and the feed to the crusher or waste dumps. Additional coordination functions are creating a safe and healthy environment through the safety and environmental legal inspections and compliance to the appropriate legislation. The staffing of equipment by suitably qualified operators to ensure effective use of equipment is a key coordinating function, together with the human resources department. Engineering maintenance schedules should also be adhered to and complied with through the maintenance system, thus ensuring equipment are available 85%+ of the time. The S2 role is key in ensuring dependencies and conflicts are managed to maintain stability.

Operations meetings are conducted between S3 and S2 on a weekly basis, where concerns and trends are noted, and synergy is obtained with S4 and S2. The intent of the meetings is directing control over the operations and supervising the coordinating functions of S2 by optimising and maintaining synergy of the activities. The auditing function of S3*, in terms of auditing and doing random checks on activities, is controlled/requested though S3.

Key challenges identified affecting the availability of labour due to Covid-19 disruptions

What is going on in the external environment?

The situation which is possibly affecting the mines is discussed below. According to the definition of a hot spot, it refers to five cases per 100 000 people. The Northern Cape is a hot spot as it has a population of approximately 1 000 000 people (with most of the population situated in the economic activities, such as the mines) and more than 50 active Covid-19 cases (Figure 3).

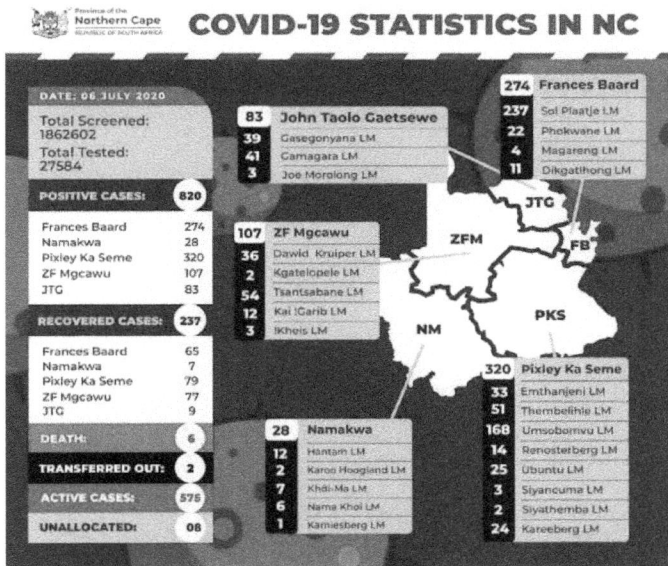

Figure 3: Covid-19 Statistics obtained from the Department of Health

Of concern is the rapid rise (Figure 4 in the rate of infections 106 days after the first Covid-19 case tested positive in South Africa.

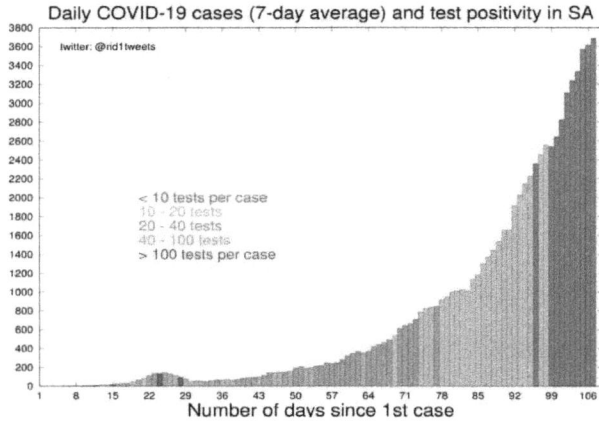

Figure 4: Daily COVID-19 cases (7-day average) and test positivity in SA

Figure 4: Daily Covid-19 Cases as supplied by the Department of Health

What is more alarming is that the Western Cape appears to be peaking, and all the provinces are indicating an exponential upward trend (Figure 5).

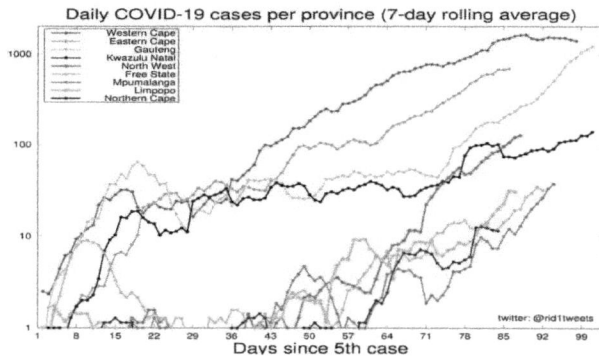

Figure 5: Daily Covid-19 Trend lines per Province in South Africa

My key concerns regarding the external environment?

My key concerns are related to S1 and the business continuity regarding the consistent supply of ore. Studies indicate that younger people present mild to no symptoms and that older people and people with pre-existing medical conditions appear more vulnerable. Given the trajectory of the outbreak in the various provinces in South Africa, we can expect that Covid-19 infections may reach high levels in the winter months which will influence statistics at the mine significantly.

Also, the limited amount of test centres available in the Northern Cape can cause a delay in reporting results and further increase the number of infections at the mine. If the mine can acquire its own test centre, it could potentially reduce the period of self-quarantine from 14 days to between five and eight days. This could significantly affect production and labour availability.

Considering the amount of mine employees and other mines in the region, resource availability (Flood and Jackson, 1991) regarding quality healthcare facilities could be limited, affecting the diagnosis and recovery period to prevent the further spread of the virus.

The availability of critical unique contractors and skills in supporting the production process also need to be considered (Figure 6).

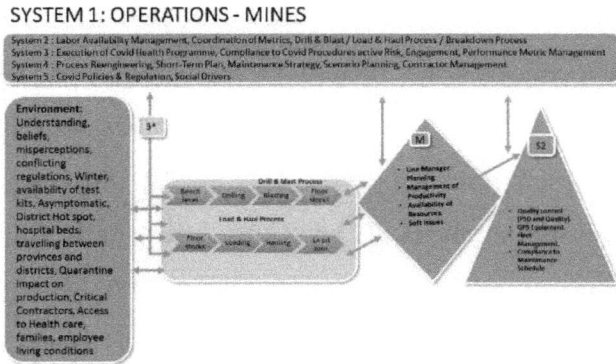

Figure 6: System 1 Depicting the impact of the Environment on S1 of the VSM

The S2 challenges are depicted in Figure 7.

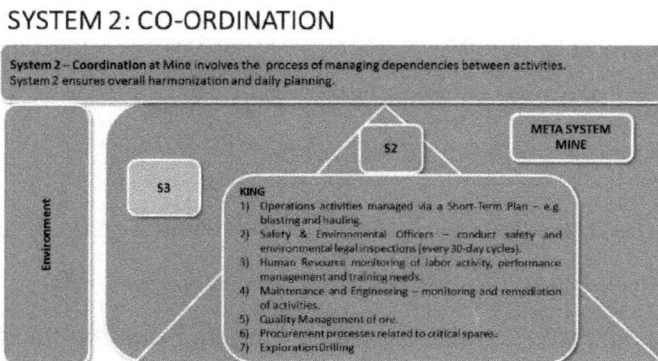

Figure 7: System 2 Depicting the impact of the Environment on S1 of the VSM

What could happen scenarios?

Planning in the event of a disruption aims to identify uncertainties and develop possible options to mitigate the implications of these responses. It also aims to identify gaps or weaknesses (Johnson, 2017a) in the organisation and enables one to take a preventative or proactive approach caused by these possible disruptions. It enables leadership to consider the reality and anticipate the storm that will hit us.

The scenarios shown in Figure 8 are some which were selected through a planning process with the key stakeholders. Although one cannot anticipate every situation, these identified scenarios will, at least, stimulate thought.

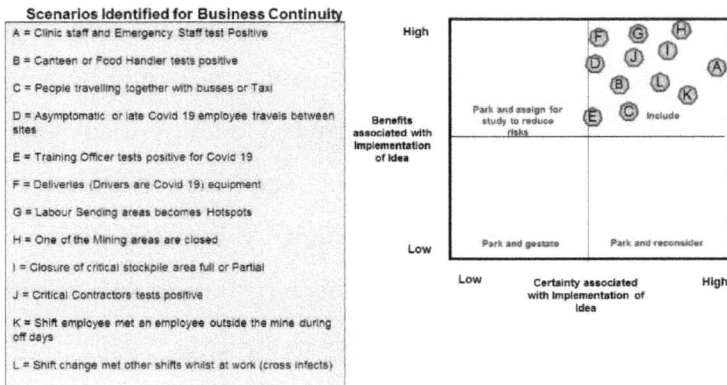

Figure 8: Scenario Planning to enable Business Continuity

What should we do if?

Let us consider one scenario from the scenarios identified in Figure 8, where the entire clinic's staff tests positive (Figure 9).

Scenario	Possible Effects	Response Process	Controls in place	Continuity Plan	
Clinic Staff tests positive for COVID19 – or employee obtains access to clinic with COVID-19	**Health Risk:** • Spread of COVID-19 to large number of Mine employees entering the Clinic (scheduled and unscheduled) • OHMP members uncontrolled **Business Risk:** • Entire Clinic Staff must be quarantined • & Contact with other Departments must all be quarantined loss of production shifts • No/limited medicals • Unfit employees leads to reduced workforce • No OMP available	Specific Response Process to be mapped	• Contact Tracing • Daily screening & temperature Control documented and Reported • COVID-19 testing • Employee awareness and knowledge • Training • Decontamination of facility	**Short term immediate**	Collaboration with other mines to bring in staff Staff at quarantine site – as backup [illegible] after 14days can return to work [illegible] 1 OMP 1 Radiographer 1 OHP 1 PN 1 OT 2 RFA operators EMS will do IOD and transfer them to [illegible]
				Financial implication	<1m
				Medium term 3 – 12 months	Contractor – contingency plan Option 2 Temporary relocation of medicals EMS will do IOD and transfer to local hospitals
				Financial implication	>2m
				Long term >12 months	Mine Closure – The possibility is greater that when the Wellness team is infected that the mine will [illegible]
				Financial implication	>100m

Figure 9: An example of a Business Continuity example when the clinic tests positive for Covid-19

Short and medium-term plans were considered for business continuity. The immediate short-term solution would be to source staff from other mines within the group. Certain critical staff were identified to be recruited or seconded with immediate effect. The medium-term plan relates to the temporary relocation of medicals to an alternative contractor in the province or transferring all medical cases to the nearest healthcare facility in the area.

What would I like?

These scenarios should be owned by the middle managers as they are ultimately solely responsible for production. The detail and action plans should reside with them so that they can optimise and coordinate the functions of S2 responsibly and without panic.

SYSTEM 3: CONTROL (Synergy and Optimization)

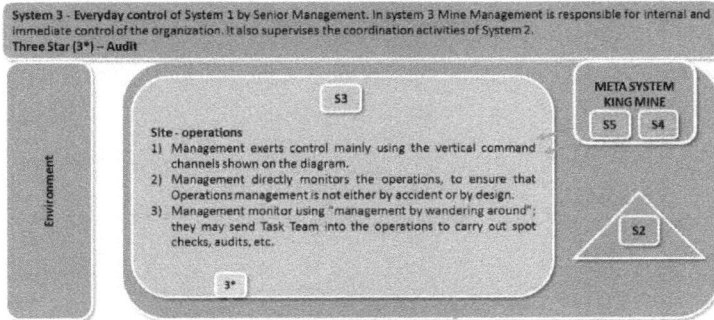

Figure 10: System 3 Depicting the relationship between S3 and S2, S4 and S5 of the VSM

Some final thoughts

The process discussed in this chapter enabled me to identify the threats for sustainability at the operational level of the value chain. The properties of Covid-19 policy application, the level of future planning and the degree of coordination among the operations were analysed for effectiveness, using this approach. This was specifically looked at in the context of the political, economic, social, technological, legal, and environmental (PESTLE) stimuli and our response to these stimuli.

We have identified gaps concerning feedback loops and responses (Johnson, 2017a), which in some instances were awfully slow and threatened the future of the mine during the storm. The effectiveness of the information flow needs further intervention and improvement. The level of variety between S3, S4 and S5 and the operations also require improvement to ensure that the organisation works together as an integrated whole (Flood and Jackson, 1991).

I also realised that S3, in its self-regulation state, requires more direction towards the mission and objectives of the organisation and joint accountability is lacking in certain parts of the organisation. If synergy can be improved through the improved coordination of services and production departments, it can lead to improved consistency in production results.

From an intangible point of view, the challenge now would be to create awareness and influence S1 and S2 to improve the information flow regarding Critical Covid-19 controls.

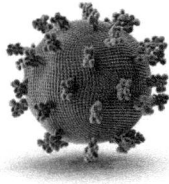

CHAPTER 5

COVID-19 IS HERE

Introduction

I cannot keep feeling the way I am feeling. I must now start focussing on what is the right thing to do, instead of focussing on what could have gone wrong. I must practise what I have been preaching the entire time about assumptions, then take decisive action.

On 6 July 2020, the mine had its first confirmed case at one of the three autonomous units. The infected person came to work from the local community during his off days for his annual medical assessment. During the process, he developed symptoms. We immediately isolated him and identified 50 direct contacts who interacted with the infected person when they travelled to work and while they were at work. A direct or close contact is a person in proximity of a Covid-19 positive person with more than 15 minutes' continuous exposure.

The same day, two hours later, another case was confirmed at one of the mines. The second infected person started developing symptoms on shift. Another approximately 30 direct contacts were identified. Two days later, we had six cases. Cases 3, 4 and 5 were direct contacts of the first case.

It is now a week later; we have 28 confirmed Covid-19 positive cases. We have identified 82 direct contacts. We have four patients in the high care unit at our local hospital. The peak for South Africa is expected between mid-July and the end of August. We have not yet reached our peak. I suspect that the Northern Cape's peak will be delayed, which is possible as it is a sparsely populated province. In the Northern Cape, which has a population of approximately one million people, the Covid-19 positive cases are expected to be a third of the population, according to experts. Our current actual numbers are just over 2 000. This means that the infections are just beginning.

I must face the Covid-19 Committee, who has lots of questions, fears, and concerns. The engineers are complaining a bout the approach we use to identify direct contacts as it influences their shifts and production. Consistency in the application of the procedure is being discussed. Management is concerned with the amount of direct contacts we are quarantining. Perceptions that people are being quarantined for using the same microwave are leading to tensions.

On closer investigation, this is found not to be true. These perceptions are however distracting me. Evidence indicates that the six direct contacts had symptoms. The information from the people's sources need to be clarified in another meeting. Meeting upon meeting are conducted to clarify the definitions, including "Person Under Investigation", "infectious period", "window period", "quarantine" and "isolation". Management's interest in our definitions and criteria are challenged. We refer to the National Institute for Communicable Diseases (NICD) guidelines. Yet, back, and forth we go, meetings and frustrations due to the impact to productivity. These are just some of the many distractions I am experiencing.

Contact tracing needs to be speedy and accurate to reduce the rate of infection. So, we complete contact tracing and further extend it based on information supplied by the NICD regarding community acquired contacts (off mine). As of 13 July, we have conducted 250 tests, with 62 outstanding. The one site has 60% of our cases. This is the hot spot for the mine, I think. But is it community acquired, or workplace acquired? (Figure 1).

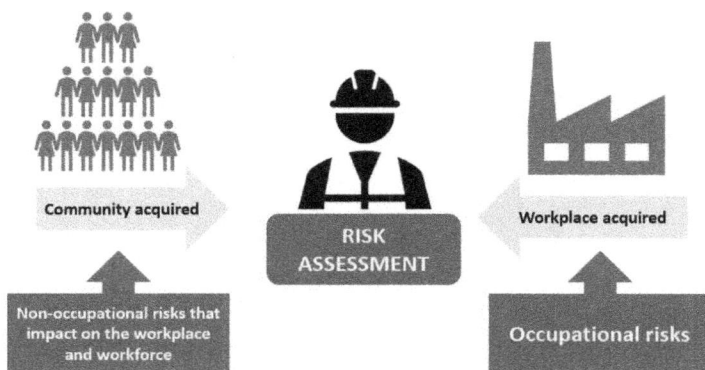

Figure 1: Investigation process to determine source of the virus, adopted from SANS 16001 audit 2020

Clearly, some more questions need to be answered through an incident investigation. I still believe that the virus is community acquired, and that contact tracing is only an investigation to determine the root cause and source of the case. Each of the 28 confirmed cases need to be investigated and reported to the authorities within 30 days as it is a serious health threatening occurrence according to the Mines Health and Safety Act.

Many negative thoughts are going through my mind. I must control them and keep my focus through this difficult time. It is our "new normal", and the General Manager says that this will be the most difficult six months for the mine. I need to focus on something good. I must get rid of these negative feelings and thoughts and focus on a message. At the same time, I need to keep my head up and speak with integrity, even when things are tough or when I am frustrated. Yet, being positive alone will not change the situation. I must deal with the real challenges and issues out there. Now more than ever, direct, and hopeful communication is needed. With a major crisis like this pandemic, I believe it is a test to see how committed you really are. I need to focus on what is working and improve on these, instead of focussing on the problems.

I need to share the news with the Covid-19 Committee and reassure them as soon as possible. I decide to create a presentation titled "Person under investigation and reporting". "Team, we are officially in a crisis", I started the presentation. Then I discussed our crisis management procedure which kicks in as we have a significant amount of health threatening occurrences (Covid-19 cases). The command structure (see Figure 2) includes the General Manager and me as the Crisis Commander (Covid-19 Officer).

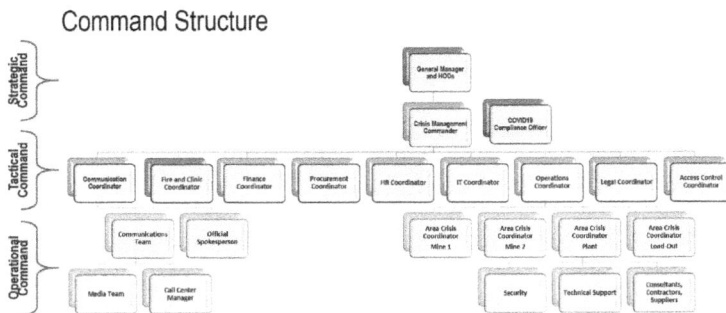

Figure 2: Crisis management command structure

We all have responsibilities assigned to us. For example, as the Crisis Commander, I am responsible for:

- "Engaging with the tactical and strategic teams.

- Communicating information to the tactical and strategic teams.

- Assisting with the strategic plan.

- Technically assessing the extent of the disaster to give input to the General Manager and the heads of the departments for action and decision making.

- Notifying the relevant governmental departments.

- Overseeing and monitoring the crisis response efforts.

- ß Coordinating the tactical response.

- Leading and chairing the crisis management team; and

- Liaising with the wellness and emergency team" (Mines Crisis Guideline).

The first lesson is that, instead of judging ourselves, we must decide to focus on the immediate situation and become conscious about our decisions. We cannot fall into the trap of judging others based on their perceptions or opinions of us. If we find fault with others or start judging others by our own values, we might as well judge ourselves.

I went on to explain to the management team that scientists will find a vaccine for Covid-19. But this is not the end; another crisis will take its place, maybe a "Covid-23". We must change the way we work, as this is our new way of working, our "new normal". We cannot keep on doing the same thing and expecting different results.

Spiritual reflection

Exodus 14:14 says, "The Lord will fight for you, and you shall hold your peace".

Allow me to give a little bit of background to these words. The Israelites were enslaved in Egypt. Then, through the mighty intervention of God, the Pharaoh, the king of Egypt, was moved to give them their freedom. Moses led the people out of Egypt to the Promised Land, and God took them on a detour through the wilderness so that they could avoid certain conflicts and dangers. In the meantime, the Pharaoh changed his mind, and, with his army, chased after the Israelites. They became aware of this and reached the Red Sea with the Egyptians behind them. They were cornered before the Sea. They saw no way out. They started panicking. They complained and murmured and blamed God and Moses for their situation. It is then that Moses speaks to the people, saying, The Lord will fight for you, and you shall hold your peace. God then intervened in a wonderful manner; he enabled them to walk through the Red Sea on dry land, while the Egyptians died in the Red Sea.

Terrible consequences of the pandemic have hit us. Many are anxious; they have pain and are hurting. They see no light and find themselves in a very dark place. In these circumstances, let us find encouragement in the words of Moses. God fights for us; let us become quiet".

I can confess we have heroes in our society, in our communities and in our mines. Due to our own egotistical behaviours, we try to destroy these heroes as quickly as possible to show we are in control. We find fault; we judge them based on our own values. We are not curious to know them better. We are fearful that we might lose our power and influence due to the strengths the others portray. We must remember here what Jesus said: he whom is without sin let him cast the first stone. Simply put, people who live in glass houses should not throw stones.

The potential of a human being is unlimited. This you must believe. You cannot be influenced by limiting beliefs or negative thinking. There are things that motivate us as humans and things that determine what we will do and what actions we will take (UCT, 2014). You need to decide to refocus and act on your goals. Your life is not shaped by others' opinions of you.

This crisis calls on us to be role models during the worst of times. It calls on us to lead when people are depressed and anxious. Your belief needs to be so different from almost anybody else you see around you who thinks pessimism is the way to go. You must look for opportunities when people are the most pessimistic to show optimism. Optimism eventually controls pessimism as it creates hope for a better future.

Refocus

To break out of a problem or a crisis you need to consider whether the action you have been taking is producing the results you want. In this case, I am facing more than 28 cases in just over a week and a significant number of direct contacts, which is affecting business continuity, are being identified and quarantined. I realise that most of the Covid-19 cases from the contact tracing and movement point back to the community. My gut feeling says that most of the direct contacts can be traced back to the taxis. I need to investigate this to see if it is true. Something is not working, and I suspect that the employees are behaving differently in the community than when they enter the mine. As mentioned previously, over the last three years or so, we have been driving compliance in terms of the safety maturity, and value-based health and safety, which is your highest level of safety maturity, appears to be of concern.

The most effective way to break out of a situation of concern is to model yourself, as Tony Robbins says. In one of his videos, he says this comes down to asking some questions:

- "What has been one of the toughest times in your life, maybe it was a physical challenge or health challenge, maybe it was a lack of confidence or ability (Robbins, 2007)?

- Go think about that situation, what pulled you through, what did you learn or what in your belief helped you through (Robbins, 2007)?"

Here, I reflect on the 2015 fatality at the mine after which I was entrusted to lead and rebuild the entire health and safety system (Johnson, 2018d). In the process, despite the challenges and obstacles experienced, we took massive action and produced significant results (Robbins, 2007). Where things were not working, we noticed that it was not taking us closer to our goal but further away, and I adapted a different approach to produce a different result. This situation strengthened my belief system and the mine started becoming successful in its initiatives. I have an extraordinarily strong team, but we set remarkably high standards as a team.

In relation to these questions, Tony defines what he calls the "success cycle" (Robbins, 2007). See Figure 3 below, adapted from his theory.

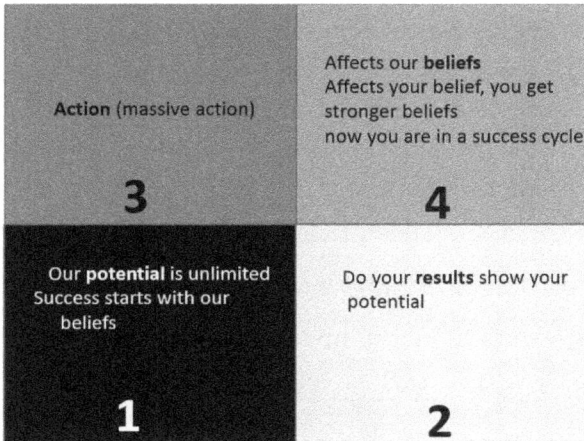

Action (massive action)	Affects our **beliefs** Affects your belief, you get stronger beliefs now you are in a success cycle
3	4
Our **potential** is unlimited Success starts with our beliefs	Do your **results** show your potential
1	2

Figure 3: Success cycle, adapted from Tony Robbins' habits of successful people

Quadrant 1 (Robbins, 2008) relates to what our potential is. Success starts with our beliefs and what is important to us. At the mine, it is important to us to maintain business continuity besides the threat of the virus on our business and our people. Quadrant 2 (Robbins, 2008) considers whether the current results show our potential. Considering our immediate context of benchmarking our statistics with the surrounding mines, they also have high numbers. The neighbouring mine has more than 150 cases to date, and our sister mine has 50 cases. Most of the other mines in the province are showing increases. Now it is time for further massive action to reduce the amount of direct contacts and reduce the amount of cases in the process. This can be achieved by taking massive action, as shown in Quadrant 3 (Robbins, 2008). Quadrant 4 (Robbins, 2008) defines the impact of our results on our success.

How to control a system?

During my recent studies and class notes on (Strümpfer, 2017a), I noticed something remarkably interesting regarding a system. If you require a high level of autonomy and control, you need to align and empower the people who use the system. Although we have been having weekly Covid-19 Committee meetings with the critical stakeholders, as identified in the rich picture previously, I need to adopt a different approach to creating the alignment and empowerment with Covid-19 compliance verifiers and employees. Fear creates inaction and disempowering emotions (Robbins, 2008). It can lead to chaos if people are disempowered by the crisis.

How is system controlled?

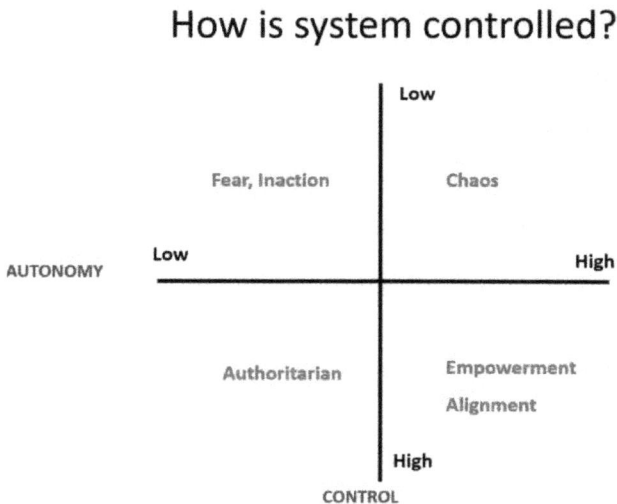

Figure 4: How is a system controlled, adapted from Strumpfer (2017) (University of Cape Town)

The Roadshows

The purpose of the roadshows was to empower and align the compliance employees and verifiers (see Figure 5). In my opinion, they now need to be empowered and aligned to further reduce the impact of the absence of direct contacts and reduce the risk of transmission both in the workplace and in the community. The current rate of transmission is R0=2. Can I reduce this, I thought?

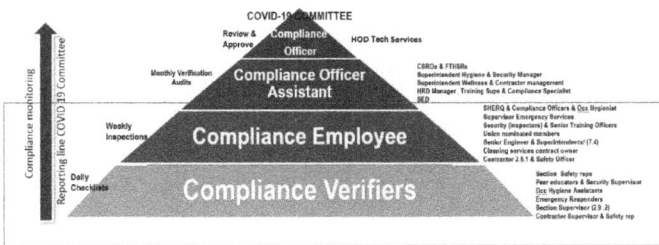

Figure 5: Compliance structure, adapted from the Covid-19 Committee structure

The expectation I have of the compliance verifiers and employees is that they assist me in spreading the message among the workforce, equip and align the workforce with the right knowledge, and challenge the employees' perceptions in order to align and empower them. This will further assist the workforce in understanding the Covid-19 context and rate of transmission; it will also clarify any terms and demonstrate the key risks. They were all trained on our Code of Practice, but interaction from the Covid-19 Officer to all shifts at the two mines and the plant is essential now.

During the roadshows, I also wanted to:

- Have a direct conversation regarding the current reality of our cases and the anticipated peak.

- Engage the fears and concerns of the teams.

- Discuss my roles and responsibility, both as the Covid-19 Officer and as the Crisis Commander during this time, and my expectations going forward.

- Clarify the key definitions, including "quarantine", "close contacts" and "infectious period", as well as the importance of critical workplace controls; and

- Align and discuss what has been implemented to date and what still needs to be done.

To date, I have completed close to 14 two-hour roadshows with huge interest and questions, clarifications, and suggestions from the employees.

It is about leadership during this time

Times like these calls for leadership which is present in the organisation. We all know the difference between managers and leaders.

Managers do not like sharing their power or delegating; they prefer doing things themselves. Leaders share and empower their people from the confidence they have in themselves. Leaders are created by fulfilling their purpose in life; they are not elected or appointed to do so (Munroe, 2011). I told the management team about a month ago that I did not ask for this Covid-19 Officer appointment. In fact, I did not want it. I discussed with my immediate team that I feel, after the peak has passed, I need to hand over this appointment to the hygienist at the mine. We just still need to finalise the management system before it can be handed over. I do not feel insecure in letting go to someone else. This is what I call leadership and it is not an entitlement, but a calling.

Leadership is about dealing with people and facing people. You cannot call yourself a leader and be office bound. You need to be out there, mentoring and training and walking the walk (Munroe, 2011). Some leaders hide in their offices during the Covid-19 crisis, afraid of getting the virus. With leadership comes recognition; we need to say thank you for our people's commitment. Let us empower and align our people to the cause of our profession and not be fearful that our subordinates may do a better job than we do.

Furthermore, health and safety leadership are not about manipulating with your power or threatening based on your position (Munroe, 2011). As discussed above it is about alignment and empowering. It is about creating autonomous teams that function and thrive when the leader is not looking. It is about being there when your people need you to care for their basic emotional needs and creating inspiration and hope during this time of emotional turbulence.

Leadership is about becoming subservient and serving others. In his book, Halstead (2010), defines servant leadership as "providing a service to others". He provides an appropriate leadership style as he emphasises that serving is a prerequisite for leading (Johnson, 2017b). He indicates that leadership ought to be based on serving the needs of others and helping others to become healthier and free. The model portrayed in his book includes putting others as the number one priority. Servant leadership is a long-term transformational approach to life and work. If you cannot share and grow with your people, it becomes difficult to adopt this leadership style.

Leadership is also about being authentic and inspiring others through your purpose and values. Leaders have traditionally been valued for their communication and decision-making skills. Although these are important skills for leaders, they need to be reinforced by a deep commitment to listening intently to others. Leaders must become great and keen listeners (not carrying on stories or rumours). They need to have their ears to the ground. They need the ability to reflect and must be able to get in touch with their own inner voice. Leaders seek to identify the will of a group and help clarify that will. Listening also involves spoken conversation and exchanging thoughts, expressions, and feelings. The purpose of a dialogue is to gain understanding and examine the differences and similarities. It is built on respect and connective thinking which focus on the participants' strengths (not weaknesses), tapping into the wisdom of everyone to develop an understanding and common ground. Persuasion and debate are not part of a dialogue. A good listener remains in a position to assess the relationship among the facts, opinions, attitudes, and feelings being expressed and is, therefore, able to respond to the total expression of the other person. Ultimately, listening requires that people be important. You need to have a sensitive ear.

Another attribute of leaders is that they must always show empathy for their followers in all situations. Leader strive to understand and empathise with others. People need to be accepted since we are all unique.

Planning change management

Since the time I wrote Chapter 1, close to the time the first case was diagnosed in South Africa on 5 March 2020, about four months have passed. We are now 120 days into the lockdown and globally there are 158 million cases and 638 271 people have died of the virus.

This change to our way of life hit us suddenly and abruptly. Change is not unknown to us and we, in fact, must live with it. Dear health and safety practioner, the change over the last four months has been dramatic. Yet, if you cannot manage change, then you should not be in this profession. For most of us, life is so difficult and still we do not want it to change. As one of my mentors once said, the only way to stop changing is to stop living. So, when one of the team members commented that scientists have found a vaccine during the Committee meeting, I told the management team that, in the future, there will just be another strain of the coronavirus, maybe an even more deadly one. Our lives will never be the same again, I commented.

We never have to stop learning and re-schooling ourselves, I further commented at the Committee meeting. We constantly have to re-skill ourselves in this area of health and safety, otherwise life will run over us. For example, before the meeting, I completed an online course through the John Hopkins University on the basics of Covid-19 and contact tracing. I had to upskill myself as many questions were being asked in the organisation regarding contact tracing. It has become the number one topic in the management meetings as productivity is affected by labour availability.

You sometimes feel like the enemy with all the changes you bring about, because people do not want to change, they need stability. Yet, you must plan your future and plan your life. We cannot change without planning. This is what prompted me to write this book. Change also presents opportunity which you would not have noticed otherwise. They say people do not resist change; they resist being changed. Romans 12:2 says, "And be not conformed to this world:

be ye transformed by the renewing of your mind." Be transformed by the way you think, renew the way you plan and think about the future of the health and safety practioner. Consider Dr Munroe's six responses to change (Munroe, 2016):

1. "You cannot resist change.
2. You cannot ignore change.
3. You must accept change.
4. You must adjust to change.
5. You can prepare and plan for change.
6. You can initiate change." 7.

If Covid-19 affects the business, then initiate the change. Earlier, I spoke about scenario planning when Covid-19 starts affecting us. Do we own this process yet? If we do, change will be easier, and we will have a contingency plan for the unexpected. Change leads to autonomy and empowerment and allows us to take full ownership if we are engaged in the change and have taken responsibility for the change caused by Covid-19.

Some thoughts to the mentees and Practioners

I recall back in 2015 I was requested to manage the health and safety discipline without any formal qualification in health and safety. Back then, I thought it was a mistake. Fortunately, some temporary help and guidance were offered by corporate and consultants. This assistance was, however, short lived and, for me, it was a trial and error taking on the health and safety leadership role. I would have preferred having a good mentor. In hindsight, I see the request from corporate as intentional. I think they had this view that, if you can manage and lead health and safety, you can lead any facet of the business. My personality is such that I initiate action and do not wait for action. Health and Safety Officers see peers doing things and re-enact situations; in doing so, they learn from experience. They do not wait for someone to tell them what to do, they do something and learn from their mistakes. The intangibles of health and safety leadership are not something you learn in a textbook; you learn them during your growth in the field.

I had a manager once who told me to make decisions, even if it was wrong. But we need to be honest when we correct perceived decisions that were taken wrongly. We need to provide honest feedback with praise. Get your people's input as you cannot live by instruction only.

Remain close to your mentor for guidance, assistance, learning and role modelling. Ask yourself: Where am I going? Why do I exist? You will then get a perspective of your vision. Determine your values and live according to your beliefs and values and your life will be more rewarding. If you allow your values to come into conflict, you will feel disempowered. It takes courage to stand up and tell others what you believe, but it is extremely rewarding.

After every significant experience in your life, reflect on your thoughts and feelings and the assumptions you have about that situation (UCT, 2014).

Add meaning to your work to increase your fulfilment and satisfaction. Determine your personal strengths and improve on these and, in so doing, you will leave a legacy.

Closing thoughts to the Covid-19 Committee

Good luck, the storm has arrived. Dress warm and get enough rest. Let us not lower our immune system. Drink lots of fluids and eat healthily. Be careful of the wandering mind: Become calm, meditate, or pray for inner peace. Let us now put into practice what we implemented over the last three to four months.

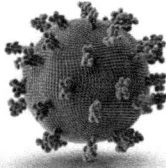

CHAPTER 6

SHOWING UP WHEN THINGS ARE TOUGH!

Good morning. For those that do not know me, my name is Andre Johnson. I am the Technical Services Manager for the mine, and I am the Covid-19 Officer, I opened the roadshow. You have probably read in the management briefs that I have been appointed as the Covid-19 Officer. The purpose of this session is just to engage you regarding the Covid-19 pandemic.

Although the number of Covid-19 cases is decreasing, I honestly have my reservations regarding the situation in the Northern Cape. The peak in the Northern Cape is only expected in September mainly due to province's small population of 1 million people in the country's largest province. Compared this to Gauteng's nearly 15 million people in the smallest province. Naturally, I would furthermore expect certain areas in the Northern Cape, such as the JTG District, to have a higher rate of Covid-19 cases due to the amount of people situated there for employment reasons. The major mines in the province, which employ large amounts of people, are also situated in the more densely populated areas.

Yet, nationwide, level 2 of the lockdown has been implemented. This means we again need to adjust our system; every time new regulations are passed, things change. So, currently under the Disaster Management Act, I am the appointed Covid-19 Officer, at least until the act is cancelled. And, as indicated by the president, the act will be reviewed again by the middle of September (Notice, 2020). It should be noted that, if the lockdown had not been implemented, the number of casualties would have been much higher in South Africa.

Since the start of the pandemic, the mine has implemented many procedures, including the start-up procedures and screening procedures. These were implemented to reduce the impact of Covid-19 in the workplace. Since we started the work, we have received guidelines from the National Institute of Communicable Diseases (NICD), the World Health Organisation (WHO), the Department of Mineral Resources and the transport department. There have been many regulation changes. Personally, I have never seen as many regulation changes as I have over the last four to five months in South Africa. It has been so hectic that somebody even asked me this morning, "Andre, how do you cope because you are still looking after other departments?" I would not wish anyone to be in the position I am in now.

So, I started the roadshows to engage you on what we have implemented to date and to clarify any uncertainty. There is still a lot of ambiguity and so many questions are asked. We recently received about 40 different questions from the people all over the mine. We are still busy answering those questions, but I decided to come from the management building and personally engage the people regarding what we have implemented. I have also written this book and this chapter is specifically addressed to all the compliance employees and compliance verifiers, namely all the health and safety compliance officers, occupational hygienists, compliance employees and full-time health and safety representative as well as the supervisor emergency services, security inspectors, senior training officers, union nominated members, senior engineers, and superintendents.

I will first talk about the South African Covid-19 roadmap. I will also talk about the mine's response to the legislation introduced by the South African government.

On 5 March 2020, the first Covid-19 positive case was diagnosed in South

Africa. On 11 March, the WHO declared it a pandemic. Then, on 13 March, the president declared a national state of disaster; we all remember that Sunday night vividly. The president also announced a 21-day lockdown under level 5.

With every event, the government responded. For example, when the WHO declared it a pandemic, the president banned travelling from international countries and closed all the ports of entry; he banned all gatherings with more than 100 people in attendance; he closed the schools; and he placed restrictions on restaurants and taverns. The mine had to respond to these changes. For example, we started sharing the first Covid-19 information. I remember the first time I shared information with the management teams; at that time, there were only 130 cases in China, and I showed them how the virus was spreading in China.

The first thing that we changed at the mine was disabling the biometrics at the gates. We also allowed disposable straws for the mine workers to blow in the alcohol blower. Next, we published the Covid-19 strategic procedure and hygiene procedure which we felt were relevant at that time. We made the wearing of face masks compulsory at the mine before the government passed the same regulation for the country. The union then took the government to court with the outcome being that a code of practice for Covid-19 was mandatory. Also, with the implementation of level 3 of the lockdown, we responded with certain outcomes. These include the establishment of the quarantine facility and undertaking a paperless risk assessment, using technology as a base.

So, as the Covid-19 Officer, I had to respond to these significant events. Yet, while waiting for something significant to happen from the government's side, we also needed to be proactive to have an edge. For example, we are not required to have a Covid-19 lab. The government does, however, ask for "rigorous screening" to be in place. You need to be an active listener and respond with the best interests of the business at heart.

Consider the use of paper as an example. A lot of paper is used in the form of permit applications, pre-starts, pre-job risk assessments and so on. The Finance and Human Resources departments also use lots of paper. So, when it was thought that Covid-19 stays on paper for between four and 10 days, all those departments required attempted to pursue a paperless environment.

Lots of other opportunities, including using cell phone applications and facial recognition for access control and temperature monitoring, were triggered from our responses to the stimuli of each level of the lockdown.

I am also planning to visit the University of Johannesburg to see how they screen over 20 000 students entering the university. Now, benchmarking with other mines, processes and industries is the level of mindfulness required from the health and safety practitioner. We also need benchmarking due to the length of ques we experience each day to screen people, while they wait in the cold. The frustrations and time delays to get into the mine also prompt us to look at innovative ways to integrate practices and come up with solutions which we never would have thought of before the Covid-19 crisis.

Funerals, weddings, and other big social gatherings remain a risk. Throughout the lockdown, 50 people could attend funerals. The same holds true under level 2. This is because, at these gatherings, people congregate from all over South Africa which presents a risk of the transmission of Covid-19 increasing. People might argue that inter-provincial travel is allowed during level 2, but the risk remains and depends on whether we have reached the peak and the amount of active cases in that province.

So, yes, I must balance the health risk and not introduce new safety risks. The Covid-19 Code of Practice is not the only Code of Practice we need to comply with. There are 16 others. I must balance the risk and, if you look at the statistics presented by the president, the peak was not as bad as anticipated due to the lockdown restrictions. He says we have contained the peak through our initiatives in South Africa. We have also implemented certain initiatives at the mine, and I personally believe that we have assisted in reducing the impact.

Yet, the insurance companies, which are normally not that far off with their predictions, are predicting that the peak will take place between the end of July and the end of September. They predicted that about 1.4 million people will be symptomatic and another 600 000 will be asymptomatic. Some believe that younger people tend to be asymptomatic. If the relationship is true, the mine has a relatively young workforce with only 0.2% older than 60.

Also, we must be mindful that the testing strategy has been changed by the government about a month and a half ago. The testing now mainly focusses on symptomatic people. I, therefore, believe and assume that the current statistics is not a true reflection of the real state.

Furthermore, it is predicted that about +_100 000 people will be infected in the Northern Cape. The mine employs about 4 000 people, of which 2 000 are contractors. These contractors come from all over South Africa which increases the mine's risk profile. They also travel more because they do not live in the JTG District.

The president said regarding the opening of the economy under level 2 that the following regulations will be in effect from 18 August:

- All gatherings will still be limited to a maximum of 50 people.

- You can now also visit with family.

- The curfew will also remain in place from 10 P.M. to 4 A.M., except for essential workers. Everyone at the mine are considered essential workers under the Disaster Management Act.

▫ Inter-provincial travel is allowed for any purpose. You can even go on holiday in other provinces. Someone told me yesterday excitedly, "Hey, Mr Johnson, I'm so glad now I can travel".

▫ You can buy alcohol and cigarettes are now permitted. So, the "dogs are loose".

Yet, if we do not remain cautious, we can get a second wave of the pandemic which is essentially a second outbreak of the virus. Consider the curve of the Spanish flu of the early 1900s; there was a big outbreak (like the peak we had) and then two or three smaller peaks.

In South Africa, we had conducted 3 million tests by 2 August, with about 560 000 positive cases. This virus is not a death sentence. People do recover; as the president announced, the recovery rate is about 80%. Yet, I must warn you that even young people die. There was a report at one of the mines yesterday about a 33-year-old with no underlying medical conditions who had died because of Covid-19.

Also, the JTG district was last week classified as a major risk area for virus transmission. One autonomous unit at the mine is now our own internal epicentre or hotspot. Indeed, some sections of the mine shows 100% weekly increases in cases. Although it looks like the one unit is the hotspot, the other sections of the mine could easily become the hotspot. Just look at what happened in South Africa where the Western Cape used to be a hotspot and now it is open, while the other provinces have become the hotspots.

So, the mine needs to operate at one level above the government to ensure business continuity. I just cannot open everything the way the government wants us to do. Some (certainly not all) of the rules will still apply. For example, some of the start-up procedures might still apply. Be warned, I need to get an organisational perspective from the Northern Cape Mine Managers Association and I need to consider the risks at the mine now that most of the regulations have been relaxed and we are entering the peak. If one portion of the mine must close, it will have implications on our tax revenue, and it will have social impacts.

The communities surrounding the mine is a major concern to me. I suspect the behaviour of the people outside the mine is a problem. One Sunday, I took a drive to one of the communities and counted about 200 people not wearing masks, both children and adults. Yet, the Northern Cape is only now approaching its peak. I can only make my own assumptions regarding the community's beliefs.

Globally, as of 11 August, there have been 20 million cases, 739 000 deaths and 13 million recoveries. In South Africa, there have been 463 000 cases, 10 600 deaths and 417 000 recoveries. As indicated above, the recovery rate is quite high, both globally and in South Africa. But the Covid-19 test rate at the mine is double the global average. The mine has conducted 532 tests. It should be noted, we initially tested lots of asymptomatic people until the testing criteria changed. The mine has only been allocated 300 test kits per month. Should we have an outbreak, we can refer testing to another lab as we have signed a memorandum of agreement with one of the mines in the region.

Regarding the mine's quarantine, the most people we had in our quarantine facility at a time was seven. But we must look at the socio-economic conditions as some people self-quarantine at home.

The danger with this is:

- Do they have a separate toilet?

- Do they have a separate kitchen?

- Do they have a separate bathroom?

People think that if they are going to die, they would rather be with their families and so they go home to their families to self-quarantine. But the family home only has one toilet and one kitchen, meaning that the infected person possibly infects the rest of the family through his or her decisions.

I was myself a direct contact about two months ago and I could selfquarantine at home. I was contacted by NICD and I took my mattress to the back room. I was able to isolate myself at my house, as I had enough space. Most of the homes in the community, however, are too small.

Furthermore, the incubation period for the virus is between two and 14 days: hence the quarantine period of 14 days. People may show symptoms between two and 14 days, but typically only start showing symptoms at around five to eight days. The illness varies from mild to severe and can last up to 30 days. The window of opportunity is the period approximately three days prior to the onset of the disease. This is when an individual could be infections and spreading the virus to others unknowingly.

If we look at the rate of transmission globally, it equals two. So, every person on average will infect two people which is why we need to quarantine. This quarantine period of 14 days places a lot of pressure on the legal appointee if his full complement is not available. I know some of the supervisors are complaining that they are under a lot of pressure. When people get quarantined for 14 days, it puts pressure on the rest of the team to perform. Most mining companies has dropped its forecast for tonnes this year to ameliorate the risk. South Africans are an immensely proud nation like the Springbok rugby team. We do not like losing. We always want to reach our production targets.

Add to that the challenge in our multicultural society with people's beliefs conflicting with the Covid-19 story. According to me, and I might be wrong, the African view refers to Ubuntu?

On a previous Saturday, there was a Covid-19 funeral at our church. I am also the chairman of the church's Covid-19 Committee and so they informed me about the funeral. I had to inform them that night vigils were not allowed. During night vigils, some African cultures bring the coffin home where it stays overnight as part of the mourning process. The next morning, the funeral takes place. Covid-19 challenged their beliefs due to the regulations that were passed. Imagine what devastation could have been caused if they went against the regulations and the entire family had succumbed to the virus. Covid-19 brought a new normal.

The other day we also heard that the local hospital did not have a ventilator for a Covid-19 patient and the mine assisted. It is concerning when the hospital must borrow a ventilator from you, since you assume you would be safe at the hospital. But this is where corporate social responsibility of organisations stretches. It sometimes extends right into the community where the impact is felt, where our employees and their families live.

Another challenge we had is our local taxi service. Most of our contact tracing goes back to the taxis. As a young man I used to drive in the taxis. They are always in a rush and loaded to full capacity. Only when the regulations restricted them to 70% occupancy during one of the levels of the lockdown were, they not fully loaded. The government then relaxed those regulations which resulted in the taxis operating at 100% capacity again. The government relaxed the regulations because the taxi industry is important for South Africa's economy. To be realistic, the cost of sanitization between trips and loads results in an additional cost to the taxi drivers. But there was indeed a case in one of the taxis where we had to quarantine seven people. Still, people use taxis for the socialisation and because it is cheaper riding in a taxi than using your own car. I am currently in discussions to introduce a second intervention for taxis with our Social Economic department.

This will be a difficult six months for us, but we will pull through. Please let us remain focus. Please spread the message that each one is a brother's keeper. Let us fight this pandemic together as a team; we can fight it. I cannot do it on my own. I need your help, now more than ever, to ensure the controls are in place. I know people may become complacent about Covid-19. I am asking you, begging you, not to become complacent before the peak.

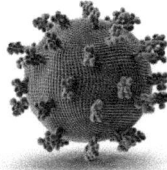

CHAPTER 7

MY EMOTIONAL REFLECTION GOING TOWARDS THE STORM

Why I am writing this Book?

Something happens when you reach an important milestone. Somehow you need to delve deep within yourself. You have been externally focussed for all your life; then suddenly you are aware of your own consciousness. So, for the last 30 years or so, I have been focussed on accumulating and achieving certain outcomes like education, promotions, home, and a bank balance. Then, while considering writing this book shortly after my sister's and mother in law's deaths in March and April, respectively, I became much more aware of my own consciousness and had to ask myself some questions. I started looking at myself, more mindful and reflective of my own thoughts and emotions. Life is made up of certain events, both pleasant and unpleasant, such as my loved ones' deaths. These events can produce anxiety through which I developed insights and discovered my authentic self. In the same way, my Covid-19 journey since February has been filled with lots of pleasant and unpleasant events.

Essentially, at the cusp of a milestone, you start paying deliberate attention to events that describe why you are behaving in a certain way and what values are affected by this behaviour. You further analyse your life story to understand why certain patterns emerge. You are also mindful of your own vulnerabilities and weaknesses, including future developmental areas (Johnson, 2017b). Through daily reflections on your experiences and an examination of your personal identity and life story, you start defining moments which affect your mood to direct big tasks to achieve directedness in your life (Johnson, 2017b).

Over the years, I thought only education would result in the fulfilment of my purpose as it used to be the number one value on my list. I have two Masters, three post-graduate diplomas, two National Diplomas, and a government certificate of competency; yet I am still not fulfilled. Yes, I still dream of doing a PhD, but I promise you, you will never find your purpose in education only. The education bucket list on its own does not provide fulfilment, however giving back what you have learned from education is a different perspetive. Your God given talent is your purpose and only it will add value to your life (Munroe, 2011).

When there is a health or safety incident in your organisation, the supervisor or manager calls on the health or safety officer for support and trust, because that officer is valuable during such a time. What I am teaching you, you will never be taught at university regarding the intangibles, i.e., dealing with the fear and anxiety caused by the incident or event. This is when the intangibles are the highest it has ever been as your organisation needs your support, cooperation, advise and interpretation (Allee, 2008). Email or WhatsApp communication does not work during this time. You need to see the people, hear them, and feel their presence as a health and safety officer.

I felt trapped in a job and a career many years ago. When I started working at the mine in 1990, I thought about promotions and retiring after 30 or 40 years. I knew I had leadership potential; so, I worked extremely hard and achieved my desired education level and, yes, I got promoted throughout the first 20 odd years of my career. But, over the last 10 years or so, I no longer got promoted, even though I probably worked the hardest and added the most value. I had aspired to become a general manager or even an executive. This has not happened.

I must, however, say that the last couple of years has been the most fulfilling as I decided to integrate my life's purpose into my job. I have given up on the career rat race. If you are stuck in that race, you lose your inner purpose and soul. If someone does not like you, no matter what your potential is, he or she will block you from progressing. Chasing your career only allows you to miss spending time on valuable things, such as writing a book like this. Schools never teach you how to realise your gift and purpose. They are focussed on what career you will take up one day so that you can reach a certain level of prosperity.

If you find your purpose, then you will find your gift and talent (Munroe, 2011). When your gift starts developing, your enemies will come for your gift. They will pay you for your gift. Your purpose and gift are for others. It is for society to learn and live from.

Our society has become very focussed on accumulating external success, with limited focus on the internal. We only start focussing on the internal when we experience some loss, for example, sickness, job loss, financial loss or even the death of a loved one. The older you become, the more you focus on becoming or being than on doing (Sewchurran, 2018).

Covid-19 awakens your consciousness

Various levels of consciousness (Sewchurran, 2018) were at play during my Covid-19 journey (see Figure 1).

STATES OF
CONSCIOUSNESS AS A
HUMAN BEING BUILDS
COMPETENCE

Unconscious Incompetence — dont know what you dont know

Conscious Incompetence — Aware of what you dont know

anxious
nervous
stressing
trashing
break-down
(mind-body disunity)

dissonance

Conscious competence — aware of activity focussed conscious of what the goal is conscious of desired effect aware of whats at play What is known as thinking

Unconscious Competence — walking, climbing stairs, surfing the net, reading, watching TV

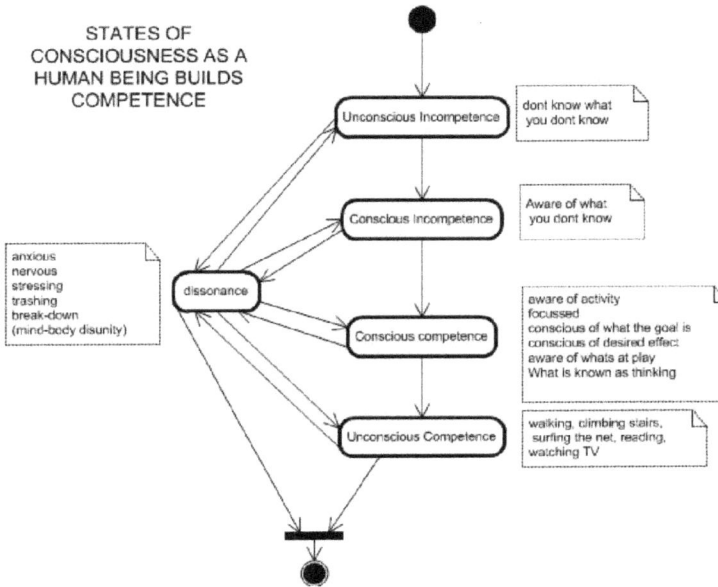

Figure 1: Dimensions of consciousness, adapted from EMBA, 2017 class notes (Everydayness)

The first concept of consciousness concerns dissonance which deals with anxiety, stress, and nervousness. I must admit that during the forthcoming crisis, there was a lot of anxiety from top management down to the lower levels, even before the first Covid-19 positive case at the mine or in our province. Dissonance is very intricately linked to conscious incompetence which we all experienced at the beginning of the crisis or certainly experienced after the president made his first announcement on 15 March 2020. Our conscious incompetence became even worse when we heard the military was coming and all the regulations were passed. The whole country went panic shopping, checked our wills and were in total silence the first couple of weeks of the lockdown.

The same happened in our organisation. During this time, I realised that I did not know everything and as a team we counted on each other to coach each other, interpret the situation, and clarify the concepts continuously. We had many meetings, while South Africa was in lockdown. Lots of mistakes were made and there were many misinterpretations of concepts, but this only became clear as we made more inquiries and researched the concepts further. At the same time, management expected me to know everything and to advise and lead as the Covid-19 Officer. So, I recently completed an online course through the John Hopkins University on contact tracing as this concept was causing a huge amount of conflict and misunderstanding as more employees were quarantined. I started roadshows to clarify to the compliance employees and compliance verifiers the concepts and initiatives we have implemented since March 2020 in preparation for the storm.

Another state of dissonance is unconscious competence. This concerns the things you do unknowingly example changing the gears whilst driving. So, you are unaware that some experience or intuition is leading you to do the right thing. At first, our team had unconscious incompetence. But, with the assistance of the Covid-19 Committee, literature, various sources of legislation and other guidance, we became more focussed and aware and thus conscious competent.

To come back to myself, I am turning 50 next month and so I have started focussing on *doing* rather than *being* and have become more in contact with my own internal self. So, my advice to the health and safety practitioner is to be aware of this model of consciousness and to not wait until you are too old to determine your level of consciousness and the competence of your organisation. I must also advise that ego-centric people (and yes, I have experienced many of them) find it difficult to move between these levels of consciousness, but you must open yourself to your own spirituality. Hence, in this book, you will find many spiritual references or foundations which I refer to. These have kept me grounded during the forthcoming storm; I had to remain calm and in control.

In my career life, I have experienced that a health and safety system will fail if the health and safety practitioner lack a depth of value or does not live up to the standards of others' expectations. Also, due to the inherent structure of the Mine Health and Safety Act, the legal appointments at mines give more balance of power to top management. This causes health and safety practitioners to not fully express their purpose regarding health and safety. They are sometimes too concerned about their job security to express their beliefs. So, their intelligence is lost due to the imbalance of power caused by authority.

If you encounter a challenge or negative reactions to an idea, then ego is present (Johnson, 2017b). When you identify and address this, you will find that there will be fewer challenges. Sometimes, we also do not want to create enemies. The stronger the ego, the stronger the enemy will be. Newton said that for every action there is an equal and opposite reaction. The only reaction that does not oppose health and safety is one that aims at the greater good. As a health and safety practitioner or business leader, you need to consider the needs of all and not only the critical few.

Another thing I have noticed from my experience as a health and safety practitioner is that there is a lot of focus on lengthy action plans. The focus instead should be on getting the organisation to become consciously competent and *being* rather than *doing* (Sewchurran, 2018). In so doing, a health and safety practitioner will fulfil his or her purpose and destiny and leave a system that is sustainable for decades to come.

What is your plan for yourself?

Your goals begin with your daily focus and the questions you ask yourself are integrated into your beliefs and ultimately your purpose. If you ask a different question, your focus will change (Robbins, 2008). If you believe in your potential and what you want to become, you will live a purposeful life. This will bring much more satisfaction and fulfilment to your life (Robbins, 2008).

Authentic leadership deals with personal transformation and narrowing the gap between who you are as a leader and who you think you are. It is about knowing yourself better as an individual and understanding your foundations and values to be an effective leader. For most of us, this is a long-term journey. Our own thinking determines whether we are bad or not. To find out who I am, I first need to find out who I am not (Johnson, 2017b).

My Background

My background and views as shaped by my own family, experiences, and education for you to better understand me

I was born in the old South Africa in a town called Kimberley in the Northern Cape on 2 September 1970, the second youngest child of seven children. A short while earlier, when my mother was seven months pregnant with me, her mother died. Her father died the previous year. So, during my formative years, my mother was mourning her loss. I felt completely alone and emotionally abandoned. I was always looking for love and affection as a child.

I remember as a child not being one of the seven close and favourite children. I was even bullied by my elder brother when my father was not at home. After returning from school, my brother would tell me to remove my shoes and remain outside the house until my father returned from his first shift at 3 P.M. Only then would my brother allow me to enter the house. When my father left again at 6 P.M. for his next shift, the bullying would continue. Sometimes, I had to leave the house again at night and only come back at 11 P.M. when my father returned for my safety and security. This allowed me to learn independence from an incredibly young age. It also created a great interest in me in the behaviour of people and my strong gut feeling regarding human emotions and first impressions.

As a child I was also criticised for my appearance; I had big teeth and my hair was too thick as compared to my siblings. This caused me to become overly sensitive to criticism and judgement. I had to go through a real period of self-discovery to find other reasons for appreciating myself. How you see yourself is more important than how others see you. The lockdown during the Covid-19 crisis has created further opportunity for self-reflection. Self-reflection on who you are and where you are going.

My father was a waiter at a hotel for over 40 years. He worked exceptionally long hours every day, working two shifts each day, Monday to Sunday. We lived off the tips he received at the hotel as his salary was barely enough to put seven children through school and pay the rent on our home in the township. I still remember that when my father came home from work at about 11 P.M., he always checked in on me in my room to see if I was sleeping. My mother was a till operator at OK Bazaars and worked from 7 A.M. to 6 P.M. daily. She too cared for her seven children and made significant sacrifices for us. Working this hard to put food on the table, they were not there for us as parents.

Over the years I have done a lot of self-discovery and now appreciate my parents' commitment and dedication towards their work and family. I still wish my mother and I had a closer relationship since I have never felt I could share my calling or purpose with her. I confronted my mother 13 years, after my father's death, ago about this. I felt she was treating me differently to my siblings. I do not blame my parents, as they too have weakness as we all do.

The biggest gift my parents gave me was commitment, even though my mother does not know this side of me. Thank you for everything you did for me and your advice, sacrifices and guidance. Thank you for being my parents despite your shortcomings. I pray and even bless you and ask that peace be with you. I have forgiven you and have accepted what has happened to me. It made me sharp and wiser. I know great things are still going to happen to me. I have no regrets. I do not hold any grudges. But I am also not saying that I will never think about what happened in my youth. Forgiveness takes away the pain and allows me to be free.

Township life was not easy. Back in the days, group segregation was still in place and the socio-economic conditions were hard. For example, we were only able to go on a holiday once when my father took us to the sea for the first time in my life. This was a tremendous experience for me, as my father was born in Mossel Bay and I always dreamed of going there. I always dreamed of going back to the sea. This is now my retirement goal. The socio-economic conditions pushed the community into gangsterism and school dropouts. For example, at first, for pocket money, I worked in the backyard and washed cars for the white people every Saturday. As I grew older, I started going out on the streets, trying to make a living with friends.

I formed my own gang and became the leader at the age of 15. The community was thriving on gangsterism and this was one way to protect yourself and survive. At one time my gang even planned to rob a bank; this fortunately never happened. Sometimes, we would purchase alcohol with our money and had great times over the weekends, which sometimes even led to fights with other gangs in our community. I was never into drugs, even though most of my friends were.

Despite participating in these bad things with my friends, I was still going to church regularly as my parents were God fearing people and raised us with strict Christian values. My mother ensured that we went to church every Sunday, and to Monday and Wednesday's religious instructions classes, and to Friday's youth gatherings. My parents were obviously unaware of the double life I was leading. I must admit that I was inspired by two of our church leaders whose faith and steadfast life mostly impressed me. They also kept us captivated during divine services and showed their love for their neighbours. I started realising that I too had special values and talents, as my friends would always come to me for advice.

Neither of my parents had a formal qualification. Yet, they valued education. They inspired us through their hard work and commitment. So, despite growing up in a poor and humble home and despite 90% of my friends not making it to what was then Standard 8 (Grade 10), I knew I would be something one day; I wanted something better for my life. I recall dreaming of having a good job, an education, and a better home, while admiring how the white people in Carters Glen and Monument Heights used to live. I promised myself that I would have a good education and would be independent one day. So, it is no surprise to me that over the last 30 years, I have achieved a qualification through some institution every five years. In fact, I recently graduated from business school.

I was probably 16 years old when I first started working hard to achieve these dreams. In Standard 8, my Biology teacher noticed that I had a lot of potential. She encouraged me and, within a term, I quickly improved from the tenth highest grade in the class to the second highest for Biology and Physics. This was quite an achievement since there were three English Standard 8 classes. A year later, I was moved to the class where the doctors and lawyers were groomed. In fact, when I grew up, I wanted to be a dentist or a lawyer. Who would have thought that I would end up in the mines, at least for the last 30 years or so?

Unfortunately, one of my friends were sent to prison for stabbing (murdering) another person. My other friends started dropping out of school and were addicted to drugs. I realised I had to distance myself from such bad influences to pursue my newly found dream. I also read Gayton McKenzie's *The Choice* which further inspired me to get an education and improve my current quality of life.

I also started participating in rugby and athletics; however, my parents were never there for sporting events. In Standard 9, my other marks started improving as well. Soon I was elected as prefect for Standards 9 and 10. This showed me my leadership potential at the age of 16 and was a defining moment in my life. In the meantime, I got confirmed and increased my participation in church activities. By the time I was 17, I had become involved in the church's youth programme, Sunday school and its choir.

After matriculating in 1988, my parents did not have money to send me to university. I had a feeling that they thought I would not make it. Extraordinarily little opportunities were available for career advancement and segregation was still rife. So, I went with only 38 rand in my pocket to look for work in Johannesburg.

I got my first job at the blood bank, working as a technician. I knew this was just temporary, as I was still passionate about my goal to be independent and successful and kept on looking for opportunities to pursue my future. I was willing to work hard, making many sacrifices and sometimes working 24-hour shifts. I always saved twenty percent of my salary no matter what the situation was.

I then received a scholarship at the mine to study towards a National Diploma. I worked awfully hard to make full use of this opportunity. I completed my National Diploma and National Higher Diploma at this company. I completed another two degrees during this period and was promoted several times into various leadership positions.

I later had another defining moment when I encountered a man who was the rector and leader of a congregation which I attended for about five years. He bestowed many responsibilities upon me and trusted me to assist him in running the rather huge congregation of approximately 400 members. I looked after the church's youth and Sunday school. I remained close to him as I was really impressed with his public speaking abilities. Even though he too came from a poor family, people loved him, and he committed all his time to the Lord's work.

After that, I was asked to take on the leadership role of two other congregations, namely Ikageng and Promosa, as there was no one else to assist. These congregations were situated approximately 50 km from our house, and we had to make a lot of sacrifices, both naturally and spiritually, to make the work of God a success at these congregations. At times, I left home at 6 A.M., served in the one congregation at 8 A.M., served holycommunion and visited families, and then commenced another service at 11 A.M. I used to return home at 4 P.M. each Sunday. During the week, I did similar activities every second day. My wife and children were incredibly supportive during this time and so I managed to develop the congregations into two strong vibrant congregations with my leadership and empathy abilities.

I was also asked to take up the leadership role at a 57-year-old congregation. This congregation of about 100 members did not have a church building of their own. My family and I once more made a lot of sacrifices and managed to build a church with the help of the community. I headed up this project.

In the meantime, I achieved a certificate in Ministry and Community Service at UNISA. This achievement was very fulfilling, as I could now apply my knowledge in my community work and youth development.

In 2015, I relocated to Kathu in the Northern Cape. Since then, I have come to a point in my life where my values of living a balanced and authentic life can be realised. I am now the rector of a 143-member congregation about 40 km from my home. Poverty and unemployment are high in the community, but I currently provide spiritual care to the congregation, including welfare activities and caring for the youth. Every second day I travel to the community to support the families. I have dialogue sessions with the congregation and youth specifically twice a month and conduct divine services on Sundays and Wednesdays.

Thus, I have been working part time in the ministry, serving the young people, working at Sunday school, working with the congregation, and teaching to build God's work due to my spiritual foundations. I am doing this to have some meaningful impact on society and the world and develop my inner purpose. At work, I practice high levels of empathy in my attempt to make a difference to society and community through care and love. I also enjoy mentoring sessions at work.

While being Covid-19 Officer, I have also been the Northern Cape Covid-19 Chairman of a committee which deals with the return to church. We have been preparing 86 congregations to return to church, after the regulations were published. So, every Sunday and sometimes during the week, I am the chairman of the Covid-19 Committee at church, advising, preparing, and training the congregation coordinators on returning to church; something which I dearly consider important. You do what you do because of your beliefs and the meaning you assign to events. The actions you are prepared to take are inspired by the Holy Spirit. Your passion and purpose keep you going (Robbins, 2008). This means that if you know what you are passionate about, you can go the extra mile.

I would like to reach out and touch and influence more people in the community. The values that drive me is honesty, integrity, commitment and treating people with dignity and respect. I have an accountability to my family, congregation, and those I encounter. I am a compassionate person and am inspired to make a difference to the lives of others in the current situation in South Africa. Get in touch with what is important to you, your highest values and purpose in life. Lead from the inside out (Johnson, 2017b).

We cannot be indifferent to the suffering of our neighbours. Our sympathy takes on a new dimension as we feel with others who are dealing with difficulties or even experiencing hardships and distress. We are concerned and pray and intercede with them.

Proverbs 16:9 says that a man's heart plans his way, but the Lord directs his steps. If you fail to plan, you plan to fail. My first documented plan was written when I was 20 years old on a little pink piece of paper. I still have that paper and have achieved 99% of my goals. The magic of writing down your goals is that your goals start to grow. During Covid-19, we wrote down goals for the system we had to implement each week. We did not write down the emotional and intangible issues. Yet, these had the potential of derailing the entire system. As you document your goals, they expand into better and improved outcomes (Robbins, 2008).

Our Social and Ethical Responsibility caused by Covid-19?

This book looks at social responsibility. What were my motivations and perspectives on my social and ethical responsibility caused by Covid-19 (Johnson, 2018c)**?**

I will address this question from a mining perspective, but it can equally be applied to any organisation affected by Covid-19.

In my view, the biggest role Covid-19 had, in terms of social responsibility, is the legislation around mining in South Africa and its impact on the surrounding communities. The issue for me is the cost of compliance (regarding the various legislation pieces being published), the uncertainty affecting investor confidence and the ability for companies to be sustainable in the future. However, I do realise that to survive we cannot turn a blind eye and only focus on excessive margins; we have a role to play in influencing the macroeconomic environment. The mines in the province have invested a substantial amount in the Department of Health for Personal Protective Equipment, beds, community Covid-19 testing and job creation.

What exacerbates the current situation of inequality and poverty is the political uncertainty, the fights within the parties, and the lack of respect politicians and the private sector have regarding fraud and corruption. Based on media coverage, I understand that funds allocated for Covid-19 relief are being stolen. The implication of such corruption was seen in the recent downgrade of the South African currency which will now affect South Africa's ability to pay its debts as a country. The situation is further exacerbated by the low economic growth in South Africa. This affects investor confidence because the economy is not growing. This is one of the reasons why the lockdown regulations have been relaxed to allow the economy to open. The relaxation of the lockdown now places significant pressure on the mining houses to implement health initiatives and take on a bigger social responsibility (for example, the recent Mandatory Code of Practice for Covid-19 and HIV and TB).

In a capitalistic system, this social responsibility goes against our policy of labour productivity and cost efficiency; it goes against our competitiveness of being a global player (Johnson, 2018c). Competitiveness in the global market does not match our social responsibility and cost of compliance in South Africa. Yet, we know we must improve our social responsibility.

Some mining companies cannot handle the social responsibility and have decided to look for growth outside South Africa (Johnson, 2018b). Policy certainty allows us to predict cash flow certainty. In South Africa and elsewhere, this is difficult to do. Every year there is a new levy (for example, levy for carbon). We experience electricity tariff increases due to the poor management of the power facility and the lack of infrastructure on the water system directly affects our ability to grow in the Northern Cape. Companies are feeling the impact of this on their bottom line.

Companies also realise that they cannot sustain their cash flow and there is, therefore, a need to be innovative by considering technology and productivity improvements to balance the impact of social responsibility on businesses

(Johnson, 2018c). Social responsibility and ethics, together with balancing the cash flow through integration, will become a key function of a Chief Executive Officer (CEO).

The one force becoming stronger is unemployment. We are socially responsible for creating jobs. This need to create jobs will remain a significant issue post Covid-19. Challenges and expectations from most governments and society is to provide more jobs, ensure a cleaner environment and invest in countries. It will be a healthier environment.

A further consideration is that society now has a larger voice through social media. If not managed, social media messages can wipe out market capitalisation and reputation in a twinkle of an eye. CEOs need a different skill set and need to have the capability to balance ethics, macro-economic issues, and business plans to be more integrated to serve the needs of the many (Johnson, 2018c).

The questions now become:

- Is a company's business strategy aligned with the transition to societal responsibility?

- Have we acknowledged these changes?

- Are we building the capacity?

- Is our strategy integrated into our operational decision making and business models?

Maintaining our social licence to operate converts into a different paradigm of maintaining our social and relationship capital. This requires an alignment with the sustainable developmental goals, adopting environmental stewardship and operational performance.

How can we be social partners by working with government to influence policy making and working directly with communities to uplift the communities? This can be the start of creating shared value with employees and communities (Johnson, 2018c).

Conclusion and learning journey

This book is a summary of my life story, values and beliefs and a reflection of my Covid-19 journey. It started with a concern related to the lockdown and the forthcoming Covid-19 storm.

Considering the context of Covid-19 and the recent increase in Covid-19 infections in South Africa and the mine specifically, this book addresses focused on how we could improve the level of compliance and drive a health and safety culture proactively.

It became clear that we need to invest in the intangibles of the health and safety practitioner including the Business Leader. There is also a need to address the adoption of proactive health and safety practices to improve the current situation of health and safety, not only at the mines, but also in the surrounding communities.

Thus, we need a conversation mechanism to integrate the leaders and workers through a health and safety partnership through proactive behaviours and a common purpose (Johnson, 2018d). The leaders must value the health and safety work and create the environment for proactive compliance, conversations for action, visibility, and support to the workers through feedback. Health and safety risk practices must also be planned and monitored and require a level of joint accountability by ensuring the correct stakeholders are aligned to the shared value (Johnson, 2018d). Senior management, including the CEO, must furthermore be actively involved in the health and safety system, spearheading the dialogue, and visibly demonstrating commitment to the workers. At the same time, the employees should actively participate in health and safety by raising their concerns and expecting timeous feedback on the issues raised. The leaders and teams must ensure that safety is not an afterthought but is just as important to production. Learning must be demonstrated daily through engagement, visible display, and commitment to a transformation into a competent worker (Johnson, 2018d).

Health and safety also require full ownership and consistent focus. The paradigm change for safe production becomes tonnes produced at the mines to be on time, to the right quality standard and incident free.

Recent trends in the industry has seen other "silent" stakeholders, such as investors, directors, and the broader community, taking class action against

CEOs and employers for not managing health and safety. CEOs are sued for fraud over quarterly health and safety promises as the impact of downtime affects the delivery of promised production, cash flow and dividends, impacting share prices. Therefore, health and safety proactive key performance indicators must be driven and expected from the board.

A high performing health and safety culture requires a commitment to relationships to improve the shared value. Numerous health and safety transactions are taking place between individuals and groups and includes both tangible and intangible transactions. Conversations improve understanding, trust and empathy and allow a process of information connectedness between departments and individuals (Moldoveanu and Leclerc, 2011). The success of health and safety programmes leads to an increase in connectedness and intangible transactions (Allee, 2008) by providing a safety partnership based on values of care and collaboration towards a common objective.

Last words

What a blessing it has been for me to be writing this book. I am nearly 50, time flies. So, I still have some motivation inside of me to write to you and give back the little I know. If there are one or two points in this book you can take with you, then I have succeeded.

MY EMOTIONAL REFLECTION GOING TOWARDS THE STORM

Bibliography

Allee, V. (2008) "Value network analysis and value conversion of tangible and intangible assets," Journal of Intellectual Capital, 9(1), pp. 5–24. doi: 10.1108/14691930810845777.

Bates, M. J., Niles, M. and Taylor, M. (2008) "Complexity and Self-organization," pp. 1–20. Available at: Retrieved from University of Cape Town, Graduate School of Business portal/https:/vula.uct.ac.za/portal/site/.

Braun, W. (2002) "The system archetypes," System, pp. 1–26. Available at: http://www.myewb.ca/site_media/static/attachments/group_topics_group- topic/86984/systemarchetypes.pdf.pdf.

Consultants, N. M. G. (2020) "COVID-19 Actuarial Modelling of the Pandemic," (April), p. 1 to 10. Available at: www.nmg.co.za.

Davis, C. (2018) "Ethical decision making," Nursing Made Incredibly Easy, 16(2), pp. 4–5. doi: 10.1097/01.NME.0000529954.89032.f2.

Denning, P. J. (2012) "Moods," Communications of the ACM, 55(12), pp. 33–35. doi: 10.1145/2380656.2380668.

Espinosa, A. and Porter, T. (2011) "Sustainability , complexity and learning : insights from complex systems approaches." doi: 10.1108/09696471111096000.

Feilzer, M. Y. (2010) "Doing mixed methods research pragmatically: Implications for the rediscovery of pragmatism as a research paradigm," Journal of Mixed Methods Research, 4(1), pp. 6–16. doi: 10.1177/1558689809349691.

Flood, R. L. and Jackson, M. C. (1991) "Viable System Diagnosis (VSD)."

Johnson (2018a) "Application of an Integrative thinking approach in designing a Behaviour Based Safety Culture for Khumani Mine." University of Cape Town, Cape Town South Africa. Available at: Unpublished.

Johnson (2018b) "Diagnosing and recommending action to improve the effectiveness of strategy as practice." University of Cape Town, South Africa. Available at: Unpublished Retrieved from University of Cape Town, Graduate School of Business portal/https:/vula.uct.ac.za/portal/site/.

Johnson (2018c) "Ethics , Macroeconomics and Organizing," (June). Available at: Unpublished Retrieved from University of Cape Town, Graduate School of Business portal/https:/vula.uct.ac.za/portal/site/.

Johnson (2018d) Safety from the Heart: Partnering to achieve Zero Harm in mining in South Africa. University of Cape Town, South Africa. Available at: Retrieved from University of Cape Town, Graduate School of Business portal/https:/vula.uct.ac.za/portal/site/.

Johnson, A. (2017a) "Diagnosing and designing action to improve the viability of a system-in-focus." University of Cape Town, Cape Town South Africa. Available at: Unpublished.

Johnson, A. (2017b) "Leadership as practice paper phronesis development practice (PDP)." University of Cape Town, Cape Town South Africa, pp. 1–6. Available at: Unpublished Retrieved from University of Cape Town,

Graduate School of Business portal/https:/vula.uct.ac.za/portal/site/.

Johnson, A. (2020) "Covid 19 Legal appointment," pp. 6–8. Available at: Unpublished.

Lewis, S. (2017) "Evidence Based Management Lectures."

Mann, C. J. H. (2004) "Systems Thinking – Creative Holism for Managers," Kybernetes, 33(8). doi: 10.1108/k.2004.06733hae.001.

Model, T. T. (2014) "the Position or Claim Being Argued for; the Conclusion of the Argument.," pp. 1–3. Available at: Retrieved from University of Cape Town, Graduate School of Business portal/https:/vula.uct.ac.za/portal/site/.

Moldoveanu, M. and Leclerc, O. (2011) "The design of insight: how to solve any business problem," ResearchGate, (February), pp. 1–28. doi: 10.1148/ radiol.12111604.

Munroe, M. (2011) "Leadership Dr Miles Munroe." Available at: https:// youtu.be/YLZ0Tkpls94.

Munroe, M. (2016) "Planning Change II (2016)." Available at: https://youtu. be/4sLsec2KDds.

Notice, G. (2020a) "200816 C19 President Message EMBARGOED." Union Buildings, Pretoria, South Africa, pp. 1–10. Available at: Unpublished.

Notice, G. (2020b) "Risk Adjusted Strategy_Government." South African Government: Unpublished, p. 1 to 27.

Robbins, A. (2008) "Goal Setting_Tony Robbins." Available at: https://youtu.be/Nmiv-rCVis4.

Robbins, A. T. (2007) "Tony Robbins," pp. 1–10. Available at: https://youtu. be/ZB6yxZ5w1j8.

Schuh, J. H. and Rhatigan, J. J. (2003) "Small Wins," About Campus: Enriching the Student Learning Experience, pp. 17–22. doi: 10.1177/108648220300800105.

Sewchurran, D. & M. (2018) "Conversation 3 Short-termism and Intangibles." Cape Town, South Africa. Available at: Retrieved from University of Cape Town, Graduate School of Business portal/https:/vula.uct.ac.za/portal/ site/.

Shelley, E. (2017) "Viable Systems Modelling Part 1 contexts," pp. 1–22. Available at: Retrieved from University of Cape Town, Graduate School of Business portal/https:/vula.uct.ac.za/portal/site/.

Strümpfer, J. (2017a) "Strategy Process Design Questions." University of Cape Town, Cape Town South Africa. Available at: file:///C:/Andre Johnson/Personal/MBA/University of Cape Town/EMBA 2017-2019 Resources/ GSB4224S Course 3 Managing for Customer Value/5. Strategy Dynamics/ Conversations/5.-Strategy Process Design Questions.pptx.

Strümpfer, J. (2017b) "Theorising in Strategy as Practice." Available at: Retrieved from University of Cape Town, Graduate School of Business portal/ https:/vula.uct.ac.za/portal/site/.

Strümpfer, J. (2018) "Strategy in Execution," EMBA20 course 3 Strategy course material. Available at: https://vula.uct.ac.za/access/content/group/ 1fa6b899-3e88-4ddd-9e60-e54d8e127243/GSB4224S Managing for Customer

Value/Strategy/Session course material/Session 1 EMBA20-GSB-V1. pptx.

Taylor, K. (2020) "CLosing meeting 26 June 2020." Kathu, Northern Cape, South Africa. Available at: Unpublished Audit.

UCT (2014) "Ladder of Inference," The SAGE Encyclopedia of Action Research. University of Cape Town, Cape Town South Africa. doi: 10.4135/9781446294406.n210.

Walker, J. (2001) "a guide for co-operatives and federations," pp. 1–94. Available at: Retrieved from University of Cape Town, Graduate School of Business portal/https:/vula.uct.ac.za/portal/site/.

www.ingramcontent.com/pod-product-compliance
Lightning Source LLC
Chambersburg PA
CBHW030837090426
42737CB00009B/1008